GLOBETROTTER™

ISLAND GUIDE

Philippines

Lindsay Bennett

Contents

Batanes Islands

Balintang Channel

Babuyan Islands

Paoay Church is considered to be one of the finest churches in the Philippines.

Pugudpud

Babuyan Channel

Laoag

Luzon

Vigan

Tuguegarao

The rice terraces around Banaue are planted in March and the harvest takes place in August.

Cordillera

Rice Terraces

Banaue

Cagayan

Palanan Point

The mestizo district of Vigan is the most complete example of period architecture, especially the mansions along Callé Crisologo.

San Fernando

Baguio

Sierra Madre

Cape San Ildefonso

SOUTH CHINA SEA

Mt Pinatubo
1400 m

Cabanatuan

PHILIPPINE SEA

Olongapo

MANILA

Polillo Islands

Fort Santiago in Manila was the second fort built by Legazpi in 1571, and was surrounded by a larger fortification, Intramuros ('within the walls').

Laguna de Bay

Los Banos

Mount Mayon is one of the most active Philippine volcanoes with 47 eruptions since 1616.

Balayan Bay

Mt Taal
311 m

Mt Mayon

Catanduanes Island

LUZON SEA

Puerto Galera

Mindoro

2421 m

Legaspi

Mt Bulusan
1559 m

Boracay's White Beach is consistently voted in the world's Top 10.

The limestone cliffs of El Nido and the caves hidden within it are a definite must-see.

Busuanga Island

Apo Reef

Sibuyan

Masbate

Calbayog

Coron Bay

Boracay

VISAYAN SEA

Samar

Bacuit Bay

El Nido

Cuyo Islands

Panay

Tacloban

Palawan

Iloilo

Negros

Leyte

St Paul's Underground River National Park in Palawan protects the world's longest known underground river system, a limestone tunnel 8km (5 miles) long.

St Paul's Underground River National Park

Mt Kanlaon
2600 m

CEBU

Chocolate Hills

The Chocolate Hills of Bohol have recently been submitted to UNESCO for inclusion in their list of World Heritage Monuments.

Honda Bay

Puerto Princesa

Tagbilaran

Panglao Island

Siargao Island

Tabon Caves

Quezon

Tubbataha Reef

Damaguete

Apo Island

Camiguin Island

Mt Hibok-hibok
1320 m

Surigao

Brooke's Point

Dipolog

Butuan

Bugsuk Island

SULU SEA

Iligan

Cagayan de Oro

Hinutuan Bay

Balabac Island

Pagadian

Mindanao

Sea battles in the region during WWII produced a rash of shipwrecks that are now open to leisure divers.

Sibuguey Bay

Iliana Bay

Cotabato

Mt Apo
2954 m

DAVAO

Zamboanga

N

Pangutaran Group

Pilas Group

General Santos

MALAYSIA

Jolo Group

CELEBES SEA

Tawi-Tawi Group

0   300 km

0   150 miles

INDONESIA

Island Escape

You could expect a country of 7107 islands to offer a few surprises and the Philippines doesn't disappoint. Perched on the Pacific Rim, rubbing shoulders with the mainland of Southeast Asia, it's a country of many influences and myriad faces, with an enthralling and unfolding human story and innumerable natural treasures to explore.

These islands come supplied with all the basic prerequisites for the perfect holiday. Visually stunning, they offer a plethora of dreamy golden beaches, shimmering azure waters, cerulean skies, and gently swaying verdant palms, with the sun an almost constant companion. Get active offshore with exceptional diving, kitesurfing and windsurfing. On the other hand, give yourself over to the healing hands of a massage therapist or stretch out on a beach bed with the latest bestseller. Your days can be as dramatically full or deliciously empty as you desire.

The landscapes are strong and always alluring; whether nature's own or forged by the hand of man. A backbone of fire snakes south through the land. This is our planet at its most raw. Archetypal volcanic cones and vast lava fields hint at the elemental forces at work just below the surface. Elsewhere, limestone has been carved into vertiginous bluffs and stacks above ground, and vast caverns in the dark depths below.

Copious rainfall and hot sun combined with volcanic soil result in abundant fertility. The country's untamed territories are incredibly diverse. Seven thousand island ecosystems have resulted in some of the most specialized animal species in the world, many only found in tiny enclaves. Diversity on land is mirrored by diversity offshore. These warm waters are home to more species of sea life than anywhere else in the world, living in mangrove nurseries, plying abyssal ocean trenches or grazing thousands of hectares of what are arguably the finest coral reefs on the planet.

Philippine native peoples have been living with the ebb and flow of nature's bounty for generations, in a complex tribal society founded on animist beliefs. In the remote mountain regions these unique traditions still hold sway, and though much of Philippine society is shaped by fundamental characteristics bequeathed by its two more recent historical influences – Spain and the United States of America – the more primeval influences still echo in modern society. The Spanish gifted Catholicism to the Filipinos and 'In God We Trust' is the slogan of every devout jeepney or tricycle driver, but he'll still hedge his bets by wearing an amulet to ward away evil spirits.

The World Wide Web and the water buffalo are equally essential in today's Philippines: a country with one foot in the medieval era and the other in the wireless age. Twenty-first-century Filipinos can be urbanites with MP3 players or subsistence farmers with no electricity, but though this diversity presents tremendous challenges for the sustainable development of the country, it offers fascinating opportunities to visitors, especially as Filipinos make fantastic hosts.

Enjoy! Wherever in this captivating country you choose to spend your time.

Left: *A verdant tropical backdrop hugs the golden beach. Bring a book and settle down to a blissful day under the sun.*

Portrait of an Island Paradise

Left: *Small boats are the lifeblood of the transport on the smaller Philippine islands, and a relaxing way to get around.*

Images of dreamy beaches and crystal waters surely dominate our perception of the Philippines, but the landscapes are many and varied, from coral atolls to mountain ranges, from sand beaches to vast tracts of dense topical rainforest.

Diversity is the key to all life here. Animals and plants have developed innumerable adaptations and specialisms that differ from one community to the next. However, this apparent *embarras de richesses* has one serious flaw: many populations are small in number and have limited habitat, making them especially vulnerable to pressure from human development and climate change.

Left: Traditional outrigger craft called bangkas *come in all shapes and sizes; this single capacity version is moored amongst* nipa *palms on the shoreline.*

Geography and Geology

The word archipelago is defined as 'a sea or stretch of water having many islands' (Oxford English Dictionary) – and the word could have been invented for the Philippines; 7107 islands strewn across 2,200,000km² (849,200 sq miles) of ocean stretching from 497km (308 miles) south of Taiwan in the north, running 1800km (1119 miles) south down to the Sibutu Group of islands lying just off the coast of the Malaysian part of Borneo. It's in the top five largest archipelago nations on the planet in terms of size.

What's a Few Thousand Kilometres Between Friends?

There's argument about exactly how long the country's coastline is. The United States survey measured it at 36,289km (22,550 miles) but the Philippine government sets a far more conservative 17,500km (10,875 miles). The true figure will surely depend on parameters of the measurement criteria, but whichever you choose, it's long. The country bounds several major sea masses, including its own Philippine Sea to the east, the South China Sea to the west, Sulu Sea and Celebes Sea to the south and Luzon Strait to the north. The country claims a 200 nautical mile (370km) Exclusive Economic Zone around its landmass, which brings it into low-key conflict with The People's Republic of China, Taiwan, Vietnam and Malaysia for various tiny islets and reefs lying offshore.

Below: The shallow, crystal-clear waters around the islands of Palawan are excellent for snorkelling, having myriad tropical fish and other marine creatures to enjoy. You are also surrounded by stunning limestone landscapes.

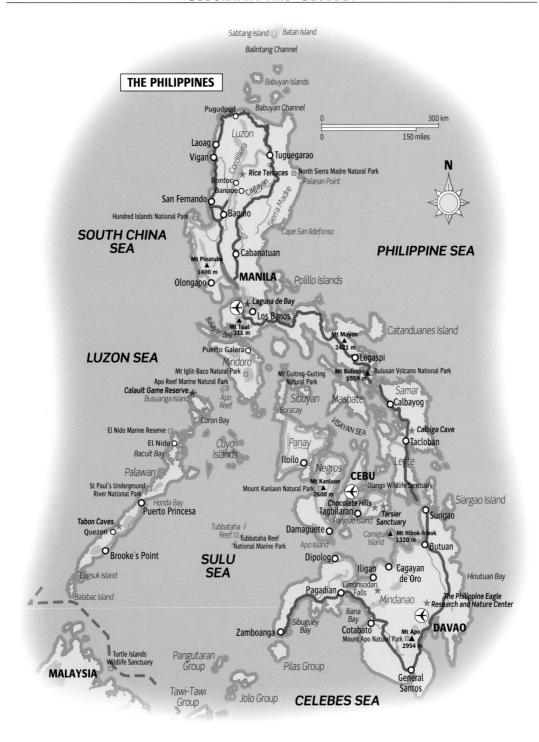

THE PHILIPPINES

Sabtang Island
Batan Island
Balintang Channel

Babuyan Islands

Pugudpud
Babuyan Channel
Luzon
Laoag
Vigan
Tuguegarao
Cordillera
Rice Terraces
Bontoc
Banaue
Cagayan
San Fernando
Baguio
Hundred Islands National Park
North Sierra Madre Natural Park
Palanan Point

SOUTH CHINA SEA

Sierra Madre
Cape San Ildefonso

PHILIPPINE SEA

N

Mt Pinatubo
▲
1400 m
Cabanatuan

Olongapo
MANILA
Polillo Islands

Laguna de Bay
Los Banos
Mt Taal
▲
311 m

LUZON SEA

Puerto Galera
Mindoro
Catanduanes Island

Mt Mayon
▲
2421 m
Legaspi

Mt Iglit-Baco Natural Park
Mt Guiting-Guiting
Natural Park
Mt Bulusan
▲
1559 m
Bulusan Volcano National Park

Apo Reef Marine Natural Park
Calauit Game Reserve
Busuanga Island
Apo
Reef
Sibuyan
Masbate
Samar
Calbayog

Coron Bay
Boracay
VISAYAN SEA

El Nido Marine Reserve
Panay
Calbiga Cave
Tacloban

El Nido
Bacuit Bay
Cuyo
Islands
Iloilo
Negros
Leyte

Palawan

St Paul's Underground
River National Park
Mt Kanlaon
▲
2600 m
Mount Kanlaon Natural Park
CEBU
Olango Wildlife Sanctuary
Siargao Island

Honda Bay
Puerto Princesa
Chocolate Hills
Tagbilaran
Tarsier
Sanctuary
Panglao Island
Surigao

Tabon Caves
Quezon
Tubbataha
Reef
Tubbataha Reef
National Marine Park
Damaguete
Camiguin
Island
Mt Hibok-hibok
▲
1320 m
Butuan

Brooke's Point
Apo Island
Dipolog

**SULU
SEA**
Iligan
Cagayan
de Oro
Hinutuan Bay

Bugsuk Island
Pagadian
Limonsodan
Falls
Mindanao
The Philippine Eagle
Research and Nature Center

Balabac Island
Iliana
Bay
Cotabato
Mt Apo
▲
2954 m
DAVAO

Zamboanga
Sibuguey
Bay
Mount Apo Natural Park

MALAYSIA
Turtle Islands
Wildlife Sanctuary
Pangutaran
Group
Pilas Group
General
Santos

Tawi-Tawi
Group
Jolo Group
CELEBES SEA

0 _____ 300 km
0 _____ 150 miles

Organization

Around 4000 of the islands are populated, but the largest 11 islands constitute 90% of the Philippine land-mass, which means many thousands are little more than uninhabited specks in the ocean. Luzon is the largest with an area of 105,000km² (40,530 sq miles) and Mindanao just behind at 94,600km² (36,515 sq miles). These also play host to the majority of the population.

In order to keep control of this geographically disparate country, the Philippines is administratively well organized. There are three island groups – Luzon (in the north), The Visayas (islands in the middle section), and Mindanao (in the south). In turn, these three groups are further divided into 17 regions, 81 provinces, 1510 municipalities and 41,969 *barangays* (loosely defined as a district or ward of up to 100 houses, or it could be a whole village. These were called *barrios* until the Marcos era.

The Geological Driver

The Philippines is planted firmly on the Pacific 'Ring of Fire', and the backbone of the country, down through Luzon and on into Mindanao, is made up of a series of dramatic and lively volcanic cones sur-rounded by hectares of ancient lava fields, topped with a mantle of tropical forest and more recent pumice and *lahar* flows devoid of foliage. To be sure, this volcanic spine causes intermittent, localized dev-astation but it bestows a fertile soil across the low-lands on which the majority of the population still depends. Much of the agricultural output is still grown on small family farmsteads with very little machinery; however, large-scale plantations, including those belonging to the Dole and Del Monte fruit companies, blanket vast swathes of Mindanao and currently con-stitute 16% of all cultivated land.

Only the far west of the country evades the volcano's hot and sulphurous breath, but chemistry still plays a pivotal part in the plot. Palawan is a stringy finger of an island pointing sinuously toward Borneo, and its substrate of limestone has been eroded into some of the most memorable vistas in the Philippines. The power of wind and water has shaped sheer cliffs and vertical towers, a sanctuary for flora and fauna above and below the waves.

High and Dry

The Philippine mountains rise in majestic ranges and for every wave of settlers they presented an insurmountable barrier that protected the indigenous peoples from assimilation. Steep-sided and with narrow valleys, the mountains only gave of their fertility after a gargantuan effort by the Ifugao and other tribes, and their worship of

Still Waters Run Deep
One of the world's deepest ocean trenches is the Philippine Deep, also known as the Mindanao Trench, in the floor of the Philippine Sea. The plum line has to be let out for 10,497m (34,440ft) before it hits the sea bed.

natural spirits attests to the power that nature has here. Today, the slopes also safeguard the last vestiges of tropical rainforest that once blanketed much of the country, a home to some of the region's most endangered flora and fauna.

Geological Prizes

Underground, the country is rich in minerals covering a whole gamut of materials, from marble and silica to iron and gold. Mining has traditionally been a small-scale family affair but this is bound to change, and bigger, more organized business is even now butting heads with environmentalists. This is set to be an epic struggle.

Around the Fringes

The archipelago's coastline offers an array of environments. Of course, the holiday-maker's prime interest is probably beaches, and there's no disappointment here; long strands backed by swaying palms, golden coves on deserted islands and sinuous sandbanks only revealed at low tide, there are literally thousands to choose from – there's even a dune desert at La Paz in Ilocos Norte. Elsewhere along the coastline rocky outcrops drop directly into azure shallows, and dense stands of mangroves and *nipa* palm – used in traditional buildings and still the housing of choice or necessity for over three million families – act as important nursery grounds for marine life.

Left: *Scattered across the Luzon Sea, the islands and islets of Palawan offer some of the most beautiful vistas in the Philippines, and the most breathtaking beaches.*

Above: Boracay's White Beach is a tourist Mecca, with seemingly endless sand, swaying palms, and a luxury infrastructure to cater for every need.

The One That Got Away

In 1878, the Sultan of Sulu needed arms to fight the Spanish. He leased his territory of Sabah (a great chunk of Borneo) to the Austro-Hungarian consul to Hong Kong, Gustavus von Overbeck, in return for a cache of arms provided by Overbeck's business partner, Briton Alfred Dent. Sabah was run as a commercial enterprise by Dent under the title The British North Borneo Company but, without consulting the Sultan, the British declared it a crown protectorate in 1881 despite the fact that the lease could not be passed to a third party.

The lease was renewed in 1946 but when the British released plans for Malayan independence, the province of Sabah was included in the boundaries of the new country of Malaysia, not returned to the Philippines. Manila sent a delegation to London to protest, but it fell on deaf ears, especially as a referendum overseen by the UN in 1962 (just before independence) showed that the vast majority of the population of Sabah wanted to become part of an independent Malaysia. Ironically, however, Malaysia still pays an annual rent to the heirs of the Sultanate of Sulu to honour the lease agreement.

The country's hottest resource, not from the literal heat of volcanoes, is its reefs. If you combine their total area with their species diversity (both coral and other sea life), they are the best in the world, and act as a magnet for divers.

Riches of the Land
Shoots and Blooms

Of the 9253 extant plant species growing on the Philippines, 65% are endemic (meaning native or restricted to a certain country or area) and these constitute a rich repository that's really only been recognized in the last few decades. But endemic life is under threat everywhere due to population growth and over-exploitation.

The Forests

The forests are the best example of this problem. The islands of the Philippines were once blanketed in dense hardwood forests that comprised 75% of plants from the *Dipterocarpoideae* family, an extended collection of over 500 species producing excellent dense hardwoods. The trees were a source of timber throughout the pre-colonial era and were also exploited by the Spanish for shipbuilding, but have been decimated over the last 100 years by commercial operators. Commercial logging has made big money but the process has been badly managed for decades, resulting in little reforestation and a sudden realization that a cascade effect is under way. The percentage of forested land has dropped from 65% in 1920 to 36% in 1970 and down to just over 20% today. Atop the highest peaks, a few stands of ancient forest still remain and these need to be properly protected from further illegal logging.

The Lowlands
Grassland now covers a quarter of the landmass. Slash-and-burn farming techniques, particularly in Mindanao, certainly started this process but the pace quickened after colonization and accelerated at breakneck speed in the 20th century. Today, sugar cane, pineapple, rubber, coffee, corn, mango, banana, and coconut are the backbones of the cash-crop industry. Tobacco output was historically important, particularly in Ilocos Norte, but it's now declining, though the Philippines still produces its own good cigars.

Mangrove Forest
Mangroves account for over 100,000 hectares (247,100 acres) along the Philippine foreshore. This may sound a lot but the area has shrunk from an estimated 450,000 hectares (1,111,950 acres) since the turn of the 20th century. Many thousands of hectares were lost as fish farms became popular in the 1970s and 80s, but over-harvesting also accounts for many hectares in areas where mangrove is used for domestic fires.

Mangrove is extremely important for marine life because it acts as a spawning and nursery ground for many species. It is an important transition plant between land and sea, solidifying new ground and protecting the coastline against the worst effects of typhoons and tsunamis by absorbing the energy of passing wind and water.

On the plus front, reseeding programmes are continuing apace all across the country; in the initial stages, these are meant to stabilize the losses rather than build the stock.

Orchids
The country has over 800 species of orchids covering 130 genera; one of the highest species counts in the world. Most of these grow wild high in the canopy of old-growth forest but there's also profit to be made from commercial cultivation.

Below: The Philippines has a rich repository of wild orchids, and a thriving commercial nursery industry that exports mature blooms around the world.

Practical Plants

Aside from food-producing plants, Filipinos have a range of practical uses for the trees and plants around them.

Foremost amongst these is the *narra*, the national tree of the country. A type of mahogany, it's been used in housing and boatbuilding for centuries. Look at the polished floors of any of the historic houses around the Philippines and wide, silky *narra* wood boards stare back at you. Mature *narra* is now rare and, in theory, protected, and every tree felled must be replaced with a new sapling.

The coconut is a trusty friend to Filipinos, providing delicious meat and milk, but the wood and palm fronds have myriad practical uses. Coco wood is fashioned into furniture and it's used in traditional houses for roofing timbers and structural support. The leaves are made into large baskets used to carry the harvest from the fields and transport it to market.

Nipa was thought to have been the most widespread growing palm in the world, but it's now confined to Southeast Asia. Filipinos use it to thatch their traditional houses – called *nipa* huts – but also in functional basketware. The sap is fermented to produce vinegar.

However, bamboo remains top of the tree as far as Filipinos are concerned. The strength-to-weight ratio of this abundant member of the grass family is better than steel. Bamboo makes up the *nipa* hut's skeletal frame, and it is also used in fencing and *bangka* construction.

Birds and Beasts

The country's rich flora encouraged equally rich fauna, so much so that we're even still finding animals we didn't know existed. Sixteen new species of mammal have been discovered in the last few years, to the delight of biologists and the wonderment of the general public. But the Philippines is a global diversity hotspot (*see* page 38) according to Conservation International. The good news does not negate the fact that the country's native animals are under pressure.

The geography that once helped create diversity is now proving a double-edged sword. Evolution encouraged development of specialized species with a limited range, but for these animals today the disadvantage of finite range is now exacerbated by constantly diminishing habitat.

Animals

Of over 160 mammal species, more than 100 are endemic, but 30% of these are classed as threatened, according to the IUCN, the World Conservation Union. Many of the most endangered animals are small and seemingly insignificant, including the Mount Isarog striped shrew-rat and the Mindoro shrew. Tarsiers

Below: *The tarsier is one of the most unusual and rarest of the country's many endemic animals. A nocturnal insect-eater, it is so small that it fits in the palm of the human hand.*

Above: One of Southeast Asia's largest birds of prey,
the Brahminy Kite is a fish-eater, most usually
seen swooping across the coastal shallows
on the lookout for food.

(*Tarsius syrichta*) are some of the world's smallest mammals, fitting snugly into the palm of the hand. This nocturnal insect-feeder – closely related to the bushbaby – has huge, bulging eyes and fearsome teeth but looks something like a Gremlin that's been fed after midnight, especially because its head can turn through 180 degrees in either direction. Small, diminishing populations of tarsiers can be found on Samar, Leyte, Mindanao and on Bohol, where the country has its only Tarsier Sanctuary at Corella; a 7.4-hectare (18-acre) swathe of man-made forest where 100 of the animals live.

Amongst the world's largest bats are fruit-feeding flying foxes, while other species include dwarf buffalo, binturong (or Palawan bearcat), macaques, deer, wild boar and flying lemurs.

The country holds many strange and wonderful records relating to the animal world, including having one of the the smallest hoofed animals, the Philippine mouse deer. It grows to a maximum height of 40cm (16in).

Birds

The Philippines has almost 600 species of resident and migratory birds that make landfall in the islands; over 180 are endemic and 60 are threatened. The major draw for 'twitchers' is that many species are rare or endangered. Rare birds include the Calayan Rail (first discovered in 2004), Isabela Oriole and Black Shama, but egrets and herons, including the Rufous Night Herons, are more common. The most dramatic birds are the raptors, including the Brahminy Kite (a form of fish eagle) and the Monkey Eating Eagle or Philippine Eagle, the second largest in the family and the country's national bird. It's now only found in small and defined areas of forest. The

Philippine Eagle Research and Nature Center in Davao is at the forefront of protection for the remaining population, and there is a rehabilitation centre at Los Baños, Laguna de Bay.

Reptiles and Amphibians

There are around 230 species of reptile of which almost 70% are endemic. All *nipa* huts will have a complement of small insect-eating geckos, while bigger carrion-eating monitor lizards can be found on many islands. The largest reptile is the Philippine crocodile, though they are not big by crocodile standards, growing only to a maximum of 3m (10ft). It's thought that less than 1000 individuals exist in the wild.

Snakes come big and mean, with populations of both python and cobra, plus several species of sea snake.

Of 89 species of amphibians, 85% are endemic.

Reefs

The Philippines forms the eastern wall of the Coral Triangle, the richest marine environment in the world, covering waters south to the western coastline of Papua New Guinea and west to Indonesia. Of 500 known species of coral, 488 are found in Philippine waters and this multiplicity continues with other marine creatures. From dugongs (*see* page 116) to seahorses, there's so much to see. Of eight species of marine turtles, five breed here, and of eight species of giant clam, seven are found here.

In developed countries, reefs have become synonymous with green issues and preservation of the planet, plus the modern pastime of pleasure diving. But reefs provide a valuable service as the breeding grounds of edible species in addition to our pretty friends from *Finding Nemo* (2003). It shouldn't be forgotten that commercial fishing still provides an important food source across the world. Once fully grown, many fish head off to open water, then onto our tables. Reefs also play a fundamental part in the formation and protection of the beautiful beaches for which the Philippines is also famed.

El Nido

The town of El Nido in northern Palawan is named after its most famous product. Nido is Spanish for 'nest' and local people have historically made a living out of collecting the edible nests of the *Collocalia fuciphaga* (a species of swift) for sale to Japan and China for bird's-nest soup. The inaccessible crevices and caves of the karst landscape make an ideal nesting site for the swifts, but they didn't take into account the ingenuity and tenacity of *Homo sapiens*!

Coral Reefs

One of the world's most unusual and delicate animal forms, coral comprises millions of minute, simple, soft-bodied animals called polyps. Hard corals are so called because they extrude an outer skeleton of calcium carbonate which links with the skeletons of other hard-coral polyps and over time create what we know as a coral reef, comprising many millions of individuals. New polyps grow on top of the skeletons of the dead polyps, so hard corals are responsible for the majority of reef growth.

Coral polyps get nutrition in two ways. They catch their food by means of stinging tentacles that paralyse any suitable prey – microscopic creatures called zooplankton – and also engage in a symbiotic relationship with zooxanthellae that live within the polyp structure. The fact that zooxanthellae need the sun's energy to produce their own food means that coral can only thrive in clear, shallow waters where the sun's rays penetrate. To form an extensive reef, corals need waters of at least 23°C (73°F) but not above 28°C (82°F). Growth is slow at between 5cm (2in) and 20cm (8in) per year and the structure is incredibly fragile, susceptible to physical damage and changes in water quality.

Right: The coral reefs of the Philippines are some of the world's finest, with hectares of soft and hard corals; a breeding ground for tropical fish and crustaceans, and a pit stop for many larger pelagic species.

Coral reproduces asexually by the division of existing individual polyps, but also sexually by combining egg and sperm from two different polyps. This results in a free-swimming polyp that will be carried by ocean currents to found a new colony and commence a new reef. The many ships sunk during World War II are also forming the skeletons of new reefs, as the polyps attach to their hulls and begin to multiply.

Coral reefs account for only 2% of the world's ocean floor but are under pressure everywhere due to global warming and rising sea temperatures. The reefs around the Philippines have almost ideal base conditions, but care needs to be taken to stop physical damage by divers and pleasure craft, and to decrease commercial fishing directly on the reef ecosystems either for edible fish or for smaller fish for collectors.

The Best of the Best

Tubbataha Reef is the highlight of many highlights. Rising in waters in the Sulu Sea 170km (92 nautical miles) southeast of Puerto Princesa, it covers a mammoth 33,200 hectares (82,037 acres) and is an archetypal example of an atoll reef, attracting a vast range of marine species. Its low-lying islands are arranged in two atolls 8km (5 miles) apart. Each tiny island offers a safe nesting site for turtles and numerous species of sea birds – many of which only breed here – and is surrounded by its own personal reef. Tubbataha was recognized by UNESCO in 1993 when it was added to the list of World Heritage Sites, one of less than ten wholly marine sites worldwide with such recognition.

A Heavyweight Jewel

Philippine waters hold the record for the largest natural pearl ever found. Weighing 6.3kg (14 pounds) and measuring 24cm (9.5in) in length by 14cm (5.5in) in diameter, the pearl was pulled from the waters in 1934. It is believed to have taken 600 years to develop in the shell.

The secret of Tubbataha is that its reef walls rise steeply from up to 3000m (9843ft) below the surface, attracting creatures that live at several different depth habitats. Scientists suggest that Tubbataha is one of the country's oldest ecosystems, the reefs having formed up to 15 million years ago along a volcanic crest now known as the Cagayan Ridge. At the surface and in the shallows the warm waters support a vast array of soft corals, plus 85% of all Philippine hard corals that in turn act as a nursery for many species of tropical fish. In deeper waters larger species such as jacks congregate and these act as a self-service restaurant for the most spectacular fish species, the sharks.

Below: With their tranquil azure waters and glistening sand, backed by tropical palms, the beaches are one of the biggest draws of the Philippines. Here on Boracay it's only a few short steps from your room to your sun bed.

Beaches

With over 7000 islands, it's not surprising that beaches are one of the big draws of the Philippines. Whatever your mood, there's something to suit: from kilometres of fine white sand with not a soul in sight, to party strands, to specialist water-sports beaches, to tiny, sandy isthmuses in the lee of tropical islets.

It's fair to say that if you want to find the best beaches on the Philippines, you should look at where the best hotels are. Up-market resorts have pinpointed the finest stretches so it's only a few short steps from your patio to the water's edge – wouldn't want your trip to be too strenuous! Many luxury resorts have their own private strands – Club Paradise being one of the best – with a darling teardrop of a beach on its own private island.

What Makes a Beach?

The fine beaches wouldn't be the same without the offshore coral reefs. Parrotfish bite the light-coloured coral and, as it passes through the digestive tract, it is broken

down into the fine particles we know as sand. Prevailing currents push and carry the particles until they make landfall and, over time, the sand bank builds into a beach. These structures are immensely fragile, prone to movement if the currents shift, or to being washed away completely by fierce storms.

Where to Play
Boracay

Tiny Boracay is the country's holiday capital, and it's all down to White Beach, consistently voted in the world's Top 10. And there is no disappointment when you get your first glimpse at low tide. Several kilometres long and consisting of the finest, softest, almost-white sand, it's a visual delight. But more than this, the beach attracts the coolest people and the scene is buzzing throughout the day until the early hours of the morning. A host of excellent hotels sit right on the beach and the whole length is linked by a shaded sandy track off which are shops and restaurants. As the sun begins to set, the in-crowd start to gather at beanbags and futons set out on the sand for a cocktail or two. Later in the evening the bars turn to open-air clubs with the latest sounds.

Bulabog Beach on the opposite side of Boracay is almost as impressive, but its offshore waters have been set aside for non-powered water sports. This is THE Mecca for windsurfers and kitesurfers who head to White Beach in the evening.

Pugudpud

Pugudpud in Ilocos Norte, northern Luzon, is Boracay without the crowds. Hectares of soft, white sand with good onshore winds and good waves but, currently, not a soul in sight. However, Pugudpud is earmarked for development and the attraction for sunning, surfing and water sports is undeniable. New stylish hotels will soon put the area on the mainstream tourist map.

Duljo

Typical of many Philippine beaches, the delights of Duljo on Panglao Island, Bohol, remain undiscovered by mass tourism. At weekends families spend the day relaxing, often bringing provisions for a barbecue lunch – fantastic fresh fish straight off the boat being a favourite.

Camiguin

You can ride around tiny Camiguin in an hour, but this speck, off the north coast of Mindanao, is known as the Philippine Garden of Eden for its forested active volcanoes, hot springs and ring of black-sand beaches. It's a low-key place for lazing on a sun-bed eating forbidden fruits.

Honda Bay

Delightful Honda Bay is dotted with several small islets, each with its own white-sand beach and a ring of coral that really epitomizes 'tropical'. Cannon Island, Bat Island and Starfish Island are easily reached by short *bangka* trips from the mainland of Palawan; perfect for hours of lazing and sunning, plus effortless snorkelling.

Siargao

This 437km² (272-mile) island, lying off the east coast of Mindanao, has exceptional beaches along its eastern shore, protected by a long reef flanking the Philippine Trench. Since the island's major draw is its surfing, everyone's getting active in the ocean and these beaches are practically empty. Most are untamed with no visitor facilities.

Hundred Islands National Park

Only three of the over one hundred islands in the Hundred Islands National Park have been developed, which gives you a wealth of choice. Linger over lunch on Governor's Island, Children's Island and Quezon Island, then you can head out to your sandy paradise for the afternoon. On Children's Island, the scattering of cabins with no electricity and hot water offers a great 'get back

Right: You can have Duljo Beach on Panglao Island, Bohol, all to yourself, or join in the fun with local families who spend Sundays relaxing by the water.

to nature' evening or two for those who don't need a gin and tonic to cap a day in paradise.

Below: When they aren't out bringing back the latest catch, the bangkas *used by fishermen are pulled up on the beach close to the village, as here at Currimao in Ilocos Norte.*

Paddling in Palawan

The incredible karst coastline of northern Palawan plays host to seemingly myriad tiny sandy coves that can only be reached by boat or kayak. This is truly a place to get away from the rest of the world. Pack a picnic and enjoy a luxury Robinson Crusoe experience.

Fishing Fleets

On many Philippine beaches the *bangka* fishing boats are drawn up on the sand when they're not in use. The country relies on these small boats for the bulk of their fish catch, with only a few fleets of larger boats capable of fishing deeper waters. The whole family joins in cleaning and resetting the nets, which can only be done by hand. Fishing folk live in *nipa* hut villages just off the beach.

A Fiery Legacy
The Ring of Fire

All around the rim of the Pacific Ocean is a thin region of dynamic volcanic and seismic activity known as the 'Ring of Fire'. The ring arcs 40,000km (24,856 miles) north from Antarctica through New Zealand via deep ocean trenches in a horseshoe shape around the Kamchatka peninsula in Russia and southern Alaska, then heads south again down the west coast of the United States and South America, including the famous San Andreas fault in California and the old Inca territory, now the modern countries of Chile and Peru.

This intense activity is the result of movement of the tectonic plates, the surface crust on which our world is formed, which slowly grow and butt against one another causing cracks that allow deeper molten rock to rise to the surface through what we call volcanoes. Any movement of the plates creates seismic activity we know as earthquakes. Violent shifts of the plates cause massive and destructive earthquakes. Eighty percent of the world's earthquakes happen on or close to the Ring of Fire.

The Philippine archipelago has around 200 volcanoes, of which 22 are slated as active. These are scattered north-south down through the islands. There were 12 major eruptions in the 20th century, the most damaging one of which was Pinatubo in 1991.

In addition to the scattering of volcanoes, the Philippines Trench, a deep-water rift running parallel to the islands to the northeast, is a major constituent of the ring. Seismic and volcanic activity around the Philippines is due to subduction of the Pacific Plate beneath the Eurasian Plate along the Philippines Trench. The Philippines suffers around 20 earthquakes a day but most are too weak to be felt. The last major earthquake struck Luzon in 1990.

The Mount Pinatubo Explosion

Before Mount Pinatubo erupted in 1991, the volcano had been in deep slumber. There was no oral tradition about activity here, suggesting that the mountain had been quiet for many generations. But when it blew, it literally went with a bang. This was the second most powerful land eruption of the 20th century. Temperatures in the northern hemisphere dropped by 0.5°C (33°F) as a direct result of the volcanic plume and gases that entered the upper atmosphere, acting as a barrier between the sun and the surface of the earth.

Small explosions began the process on 2 April when a fissure broke at the summit and rumbling earthquakes were felt around the lower slopes. These continued to grow in frequency. After 28 May sulphur dioxide emissions dropped dramatically and scientists feared that the magma chamber was blocked. If this chamber built pressure, they knew that any resultant sudden release would be very destructive. On 7 June a dome 30m (98ft) high and 100m (328ft) across was noted in the crater. The first eruption started on 12 June but the volcano blew its cork, literally, on 14 June, with two days of violent explosions that flung debris high into the atmosphere. The mountain lost 300m (984ft) in height.

Before the eruption the mountain had been covered in mature tropical forest that was home to the indigenous Aeta (also Ayta) peoples who were some of the last hunter-gatherers in the Philippines. The population was evacuated but their lifestyle was devastated – their lands turned to ash or covered in lava or thick *lahar*, their homes gone. Most of the Aeta could not return to their pre-eruption homes, causing the close-knit society to fragment and increasingly adopt a 21st-century way of life.

Costs to the Filipinos were high. Eight hundred thousand farm animals died and 800km^2 (309 sq miles) of agricultural land, much under rice production, was lost. In total, over 2 million people were affected by the eruption, though remarkably only 300 people lost their lives. Several river valley ecosystems have also been affected and Clark Air Force base, a US military facility, which was covered in volcanic ash, never reopened after the eruption.

Following page: The Philippines sits on the 'Ring of Fire',
the world's most active volcano zone. The eruption
of Mount Pinatubo in 1991 was the second
most powerful of the 20th century.

Volcano Alert

Alert levels are as follows:

Level 1: Low-level seismic activity, fumerolic or other unrest.

Scientific Interpretation: Disruption but no eruption imminent.

Level 2: Low to moderate level of seismic activity, other unrest with positive evidence of involvement of magma.

Scientific Interpretation: Probable magmatic intrusion; could eventually lead to an eruption.

Level 3: Relatively high and increasing unrest, including b-type (low-frequency) earthquakes, accelerating ground deformation, increasing vigour of fumeroles and gas emissions.

Scientific Interpretation: Increased likelihood of an eruption possible within days to weeks.

Level 4: Intense unrest, including harmonic tremor and/or 'long period' (low-frequency) earthquakes or quiet lava emissions and/or dome growth and/or small explosions.

Scientific Interpretation: Magma close to or at earth's surface. Hazardous explosive eruption likely, possibly within hours to days.

Level 5: Hazardous explosive eruption in progress, with pyroclastic flows and/or eruption column rising at least 6km (3.7 miles) above sea level.

Scientific Interpretation: Explosive eruption in progress. Hazards in valleys and downwind.

(Issued by the Philippine Institute of Volcanology and Seismology.)

The Current Situation

Currently there is no dangerous volcanic activity around the country. Mount Mayon has been rumbling away since 2001, but alerts have never been raised beyond Level 1 (*see* above), though a precautionary 6km (3.7-mile) Permanent Danger Zone is in place around the cone. This is one of the most active Philippine volcanoes, with 47 eruptions since 1616. The mountain covers 314km^2 (121 sq miles) and the foothills house the towns of Camilag, Malilipot and Santo Domingo, with over 563,000 people living within 15km (9.3 miles) of the cone. Data from previous eruptions doesn't really help scientists, as *lahar* (volcanic mud flows) and lava flows don't follow a set pattern and could make their way down any or every face of the cone into areas of dense population.

Taal is probably the most accessible of the country's many active volcanoes. It's a beautiful caldera with a diameter of 26km (16 miles) with a 267km^2 (103-sq-mile) lake and a 23km^2 (9-sq-mile) island cone at its heart. Taal has 34 other cones and 47 craters, making it one of the Philippines' largest hot spots.

The Philippine Institute of Volcanology and Seismology

Ten volcanoes are the subject of constant monitoring by the Philippine Institute of Volcanology and Seismology. Pinatubo has four main stations and six repeater stations with seismic detectors around its cone, while Taal has three stations around the caldera.

The Philippine government set up the Institute after an eruption of Mount Hibok-hibok on Camiguin between 1948 and 1953. The Institute monitors volcanic and seismic activity, maintains a database of information and provides information to other governmental departments and the public. Today it employs around 50 people at six manned monitoring centres and at the headquarters in Quezon City.

Caves

Great swathes of the Philippines are made up of soluble limestone rocks, perfect for the formation of caves. This limestone is most easily seen at ground level around the coast of Palawan and the islands of Bacuit Bay and Coron Bay, where it has been worn into high-rise columns and sheer-sided cliffs where the edible nest swifts make their homes. However, it is equally dramatic under-

Right: The Philippine archipelago plays host to vast cave systems, many of which are only now being explored and surveyed. This immense stalactite took millennia to develop.

ground, where water erosion has fashioned gargantuan cave systems that are only now being fully explored by professional surveyors. What's certain is that St Paul's Underground River National Park in Palawan protects the world's longest known underground river system, a limestone tunnel 8km (5 miles) long, and that Calbiga Cave on Samar is the largest yet discovered in Asia.

Karst Formations

A karst system is one where rainwater, carrying dilute amounts of acid, gradually dissolves soluble rocks by taking with it tiny amounts of minerals as it passes. The rain finds fissures in the rock as it drains, widening these fissures into crevices or sinkholes. Crevices become passages which then develop into caves linked by tunnels large and small.

Scientists postulate that cave complexes take around 100,000 years to grow large enough to allow human entry, so the cathedral-like spaces were millions of years in the making. However, when the cave ceiling eventually becomes untenable, it crashes to the floor, creating the vast open amphitheatres such as the Big Lagoon and the Small Lagoon in Bacuit Bay.

Rivers, Lakes and Waterfalls

For such a large landmass, the Philippines has only 3219km (2000 miles) of waterways, though what freshwater there is, has assumed importance beyond its mere length. Historically, the rivers acted as vital transport conduits for the indigenous peoples, the lakes a guaranteed source of food. Today, an element of fun and pleasure has been added to these more serious uses and they'll certainly pull visitors in coming years.

Rivers

At 446km (277 miles) long, the Cagayan River is the country's most formidable waterway, cutting a swathe north through Luzon between the Cordillera Mountains in the west and the Sierra Madre Mountains in the east, with numerous tributaries, including the Chico, the Pasig and the Magat. This is the centre of the country's burgeoning whitewater rafting industry, a high-adrenalin ride through fast-flowing gorges.

The Pasig River runs through Manila on its way to the sea from Laguna de Bay via the Napindan Channel, a mere 25km (16 miles) to the sea. However, the river encapsulates many of the environmental problems facing the country today. Curving sensuously around the outer walls of Intramuros, there could have been a pretty waterfront promenade, perhaps with shops and cafés, but instead the river is choked with litter and the waste of the millions who live in crowded *barangays* on the banks. Scientists have announced that, at its lower reaches, the river is dead; unable to sustain any form of life. As a barometer of the capital's environmental health, it's not offering us a good forecast. The authorities will have to work hard to improve sanitation and decrease industrial pollution.

Lakes

The second largest lake in Southeast Asia, Laguna de Bay covers over 90,000 hectares (222,390 acres) to the southeast of the capital but with an average depth of less than 3m (9.8ft). The lake has 15 river tributaries and numerous streams, but only one outlet: the aforementioned Pasig River. For centuries the waters have been used as one giant fish farm for local people but this important industry is under threat from pollution and oxygen depletion.

The crater lake of the Taal volcano has almost 40 tributaries but again only one outlet: the Pansipit River that drains southwest into Balayan Bay. The Taal volcano cone has its own crater lake with slightly acidic water an average 20m (66ft) deep. Taal is home to the black-and-white sea snake *Hydrophis semperi*, a rare species that breeds in fresh water, plus the world's only freshwater sardine, the *Maliputo* or *Sardinella tawilis*, which forms the basis of the fishing industry.

Cascades and Waterfalls

Iligan City in Lanao del Norte on Mindanao is known as the 'City of Majestic Waterfalls', with 20 falls close to the city, including Limonsodan Falls, thought to be the highest in Asia at 870m (2854ft). Southwestern Bohol also has a collection within easy reach of the capital, Tagbilaran, though nothing quite that high. Mag-Aso is a pretty double cascade flowing into a rocky valley and it's a favourite place for families to spend a relaxing day, swimming in the water and having a barbecue lunch.

National Parks

'The popular notion of being rich in natural resources has given us a false sense of security.'
Fulgencio Factoran – former environment minister.

A Paper Exercise?

The richness of the natural environment is told in the numbers of species of flora and fauna on land and in the oceans, but this presents a skewed picture. Many endemic species are only found in small pockets of land,

perhaps only on one island, which makes them particularly susceptible to any changes in their limited habitats. Population growth and a reliance on the land at a subsistence level by the majority of the population are the two most pressing issues that need to be resolved.

The Philippines presents somewhat of a conundrum when it comes to environmental protection. On paper things look reasonable: 62 national parks, a host of reserves and several geological monuments, plus a whole raft of legislation giving the impression of a proactive country. But the reality is somewhat different. A lack of resources to enforce the protected status, rampant corruption within the system, a poor population for whom the short-term peso is, of necessity, more important than long-term environmental health, and traditional tribal practices that conflict with modern eco-attitudes are all problems that need solutions.

Protected Landscapes

Having said all that, Philippine national parks cover almost every different type of environment and every corner of the country. The North Sierra Madre Natural Park is the country's largest protected-status area. In addition to spectacular mountainscapes, the park covers the bulk of the last remaining tracts of virgin hardwood tropical forest. Bulusan Volcano National Park and Mount Kanlaon Natural Park both protect the dense forested slopes of active volcanoes, allowing free rein to endemic species for as long as the volcanoes do not erupt. El Nido Marine Reserve protects the exceptional limestone formations around Bacuit Bay, while the Mount Guiting-Guiting Natural Park has an exceptionally mature ecosystem which has not seen the hand of man, and includes five species of mammals only found on its Sibuyan Island. The Chocolate Hills of Bohol have been protected

Previous page: Mag-Aso Falls are a shady location for a freshwater swim.
***Right**: The Chocolate Hills of Bohol owe their shape to long, slow erosion of the old coral reef that lies beneath the surface.*

as a National Geological Monument and have recently been submitted to UNESCO for inclusion in their list of World Heritage Monuments. A rolling landscape of 1700 small, rounded mounds (called 'chocolate' because during the dry season the grasses shrivel and brown), the hills were formed by the uplift of an old coral reef that has been eroded and softened by wind and rain.

Apo Reef Marine Natural Park and Tubbataha Reef National Marine Park both protect atoll reef formations. Apo is the largest in the country, though Tubbataha is considered the more spectacular.

Protected Wildlife

Numerous small, independent reserves are scattered across the country, catering to particular species that may be endemic to a very small habitat area. Mount Iglit-Baco Natural Park preserves the last native habitat of the *tamaraw*, a small, wild cousin of the domestic water buffalo. On Bohol, the Philippine Tarsier Foundation runs

Below: The somnolent waters of the Loboc River cut a swathe through the heart of Bohol Island amongst lush tropical landscapes.

a small reserve dedicated to this tiny nocturnal mammal, which has small populations scattered across Siargao, Samar, Leyte and Mindanao.

Though green turtles roam the world's oceans, the beaches of Turtle Islands Wildlife Sanctuary, one of the country's southernmost outposts (shared with Malaysia), are one of very few of the creature's nesting grounds left in the world. Across the other side of the country, Hinutuan Bay on the east coast of Mindanao has coastal shallows and mangrove forests that protect a small but quickly disappearing population of dugong

(sea cows), while Olango Island Wildlife Sanctuary protects over 1000 hectares of mangrove, beach and foreshore that's an important pit-stop for around 50,000 migratory birds from almost 50 species, and a nesting ground for many.

A Life on the African Savannah

The country's most unusual, yet widely touted – by the tourist office – park is Calauit Game Reserve and Wildlife Sanctuary on Calauit Island. Established under Marcos in 1976, it was founded after the President had visited a Third World Conference in Kenya and pledged to help save Africa's savannah grazers. Only later did the reserve extend its remit to endemic species and today it works to improve numbers of Calamian deer, wild boar, mouse deer, crocodiles and other endangered Philippine animals, alongside the zebra and giraffe.

Palawan Biosphere Reserve

Palawan is considered the country's 'last ecological frontier,' with a rich biodiversity even within the over-all wealth of the Philippines. The Palawan Biosphere Reserve was created through UNESCO in 1991 within its Man and Biosphere Programme (MAB). The aim of the programme is to create an interdisciplinary approach to biodiversity loss and promote good practice across countries. The approach takes into account existing social and economic factors when trying to find solutions, rather than the convention of ignoring the very real human factors that affect these endangered environments.

Pearl Farming and the Green Plus

Ironically, the large number of pearl farms across Palawan and the Visayas has had a positive effect on the country's marine environment. These commercial ventures have guards and limit fishing, preserving water quality for their product. The nets holding the oysters also act as a nursery for fish species, so the by-product is that the whole marine ecosystem benefits.

The Stairway to Heaven

Loudly touted as the 'Eighth Wonder of the World', and known locally as the Stairway to Heaven, the rice terraces of northern Luzon constitute one of the country's most spectacular attractions and are a triumph of man working with nature. The Ifugao peoples (a group forming part of the Igorot peoples) needed more workable land on which to grow their rice, but they lived in the steep-sloping mountains of the Cordillera, so they came up with an ingenious solution: building vast vertical walls against the mountain slope to create a flat surface on which to plant. The terraces were designed to make maximum use of rainfall and water flow, to make farming as easy as possible in these difficult conditions.

The first terraces are said to have been built c1150BC, but within a short space of time almost every face of many valleys was terraced in an immense feat of human endeavour, considering the Ifugao had no sophisticated tools or heavy lifting equipment.

Today, the Ifugao work in much the same way as their ancestors, having maintained the terraces through the intervening generations. Walls up to six or seven metres (20–23ft) high hold the vital life-giving soil, while a maze of paths worn bare with the footfall of centuries link the various terraces to the villages and the outside world beyond.

In 1995, UNESCO added the rice terraces of Ifugao province to the list of World Heritage Sites by virtue of their being a unique testimony to cultural tradition; that they are a type of building that represents signifi-

Below: The man-made rice terraces of Banaue have been called the Eighth Wonder of the World.

cance to human history, and that they represent an outstanding example of man's use of land. However, they have since found their way onto the UNESCO endangered list – in 2005 – because of the lack of an organized management plan. UNESCO is concerned that, as the Ifugao have more contact with 21st-century life, they may abandon their traditional rice cultivation for other forms of income and the terraces may fall into disrepair.

The Paddy Routes

Though terracing exists all throughout the Cordillera region, the following areas are particularly noteworthy or picturesque.

The mud-walled terraces of Banaue are generally mentioned first when talking about the region. This is because this town is the easiest to reach from Baguio, the conduit to the Cordillera region. The terraces tend to be planted in March and the harvest takes place in

August. There are several viewpoints close to the Banaue town centre, or head just east to the village of Batad. The terraces around Batad have two harvests a year, in June and December.

The Applai peoples of Sagada built terraces with stone walls but also have another unique cultural practice. The rice paddies are guarded by Applai ancestors whose bones rest in wooden coffins suspended from the cliff tops. These 'hanging coffins' form a central tenet in the tribe's animist beliefs.

Around Bontoc, the smaller villages of Maligcong and Mainit have terraces at their best in August. You can hike between the two in a couple of hours.

The further you travel into the heart of Kalinga province, in the highest mountains to the northeast of Baguio, the further away from the 21st century you'll feel. Here it's easy to understand why the Spanish never converted these indigenous peoples; they never even made it to these remote valleys. Here, hamlets of bamboo huts sit amongst ribbons of verdant paddies, but one must be prepared to live as the Igorot for at least a few days to enjoy the landscapes. Visiting here should be viewed as an expedition rather than a simple trip or holiday.

Climate and Clothing
Sun and Rain
The Philippines has a tropical climate that is hot and humid all year round. Mean average temperature is 26.6°C (80°F), with the warmest month being May with a 28.3°C (83°F) average and January the coolest with 25.5°C (78°F). Baguio is not included in these calculations because its elevation of 1500m (4922ft) means it is generally a lot cooler, with average temperatures of only 18.3°C (65°F), but it can drop to 12°C (54°F) or 13°C (55°F). Humidity (moisture content in the air) is always

Left: Terracing creates fertile land in this region of steep mountains topped by ancient virgin tropical forest. Small village communities live amidst the paddies, tending to the crops as their families have for generations.

high; a heady 71% at its lowest around March rising to a stifling 85% in September.

Rainfall varies throughout the year, and because the Philippines covers such a vast area, it also varies throughout the regions. Different moisture-bearing weather systems affect the country from different directions so topography also plays a big part in rainfall distribution. General Santos City in the far south receives 978mm (39in) of rain per year, which sounds a lot, but Baguio in the Cordillera has over 4m (13ft) dumped on its verdant hills.

There are two major seasons in the year: the rainy season from June to November and the dry season from December to May. Throughout the dry season, temperatures gradually rise until the arrival of the rains. The archipelago is affected by important regional winds that complicate this seasonal picture and divide the country into roughly four climatic types.

Climate region one (western Luzon and western coasts of the western Visayas islands) has a dry season between November and April; the rest of the year is classed as wet season.

Climate region two (eastern Mindanao and the eastern coasts of the eastern Visayas) is classed as having no dry season, but has more pronounced rainfall from November to January.

Climate region three (cutting a swathe through central sections of Luzon and the central Visayas, plus eastern Palawan) has a wet season from November to April but the two seasons are not as clear as in region one.

In climate region four (eastern Luzon and middle Visayas plus central Mindanao) rainfall is fairly evenly spread throughout the year.

Typhoons
The Philippines is regularly beset by typhoons originating in the Pacific. Typhoon season runs roughly June to November. Normally they travel in a northwesterly direction from an origin around the Marianas Islands, meaning the southern Philippines suffers far fewer hits than the northern tip of the country.

PHILIPPINES	J	F	M	A	M	J	J	A	S	O	N	D
AVERAGE TEMP. °F	79	81	82	84	86	84	82	82	82	82	81	81
AVERAGE TEMP. °C	26	27	28	29	30	29	28	28	28	28	27	27
RAINFALL in	0,6	0,2	0,3	0,7	6	11	16	18	14	9	5	2,5
RAINFALL mm	16	6	9	17	146	284	408	464	352	224	122	52
Days of Rainfall	4	2	2	3	9	17	22	22	20	17	11	7

Right: Temperatures in the Philippines never drop below the mid-20s°C (late 70s°F) so, when it's sunny, shade is always welcomed and this colourful beach umbrella is perfect. Don't forget protective cream for your skin – a high-factor cream is advised. Re-apply regularly and especially after swimming.

What to Wear

The uniformly high temperatures mean that it's vital to have lightweight clothing, preferably natural fibres or high-tech materials that wick sweat away from the body. In addition to temperature, think about the power of the sun. Always have clothing to cover arms and legs in order to prevent sunburn (this also helps protect against insect/mosquito bites); clothing with an SPF factor is ideal. Locals carry umbrellas against both the sun and the rain. Beachwear is important, but should only be worn at the beach or around the hotel pool; Filipinos are generally conservative dressers – though that doesn't mean they don't know how to dress up come party time! Always have long-sleeved garments for visiting churches and mosques.

Comfortable shoes are a must for sightseeing and proper hiking boots for any hill climbing. Plastic beach shoes or dive shoes are a good idea for snorkelling or exploring the rocky shallows.

Sunglasses and a hat complete the ensemble.

Getting Around

Travel is an adventure in the Philippines – an adventure that can mean delight, surprise and sometimes dismay.

By Air

In the last 25 years the skies have truly opened up and it's much easier to get around by air than it used to be. Flying cuts journey times to a minimum and prices are cheap by western standards. Major cities like Manila, Davao and Cebu have modern airports with air-conditioned terminals, but many smaller islands or remote spots still have dirt strips where an overpass by the pilot before landing clears chickens and goats from the runway. These smaller fields have weight limits, so only smaller 12- to 19-seater planes can get in here; and you'll certainly share your journey with a cargo of fighting cocks that crow nervously from their boxes as the engines start up.

Flight times are short – between 30 minutes and 4 hours – but the disadvantage is that you'll usually have to use Manila as a hub; it's quite difficult to fly from island to island.

The national airline, Philippines Airlines, flies to 22 destinations from Manila; from Laoag in the far north of Luzon to General Santos City in southern Mindanao. Their closest rivals, Cebu Pacific, are a low-cost airline offering 21 domestic destinations from their base at Cebu City or from Manila. South East Asian Airlines (Seair) is a specialist airline with lighter planes operating into small airports, including El Nido and Busuanga. Asian Spirit also offers services.

By Sea

Despite flight tickets being inexpensive for visitors, they are still out of reach for many ordinary Filipinos. For inter-island travel, ferries are still the transport of choice, and hundreds ply the seaways and straits every day. All populated islands have a ferry service and many rely on this for their access to the outside world. Superferries operates a number of faster routes with a modern fleet from Manila, while Supercat operates fast catamarans between Bohol and Cebu, Leyte and Cebu, and Batangas and Mindoro.

Timetables are complicated and services can be unreliable, especially where ships are older and may need to be taken in for repair. Patience and flexibility are the watchwords.

On the Road

Long-distance buses operate around Luzon, Mindanao and other bigger islands. Expect to pay around 20% extra on an air-conditioned vehicle. On smaller islands and shorter journeys the jeepney and tricycle rule the road (*see* pages 97–98).

The Political Situation in Mindanao

The Philippines has ongoing security problems related to a fight for independence of the mainly Muslim parts of the country. Groups including the Moro National Liberation Front (now a non-violent political organization), the more militant Moro Islamic Liberation Front and Abu Sayyaf (which is said to have links with al-Qaeda but predates Bin Laden's organization by some

years) are still active and a number of bombings since 2000 has raised security levels across the country.

There are no feelings of tension as you travel around much of the Philippines; however, government troops and freedom fighters regularly clash in parts of Mindanao, and threats have been made against foreigners. Travel advisories currently warn against travel to this area, so take advice before you make any travel plans.

Below: Huge buildings line the avenues of the chic Makati district. This is Manila's key business, commercial and shopping district.

Island Culture

Left: Motor-tricycles wait for passengers at Cagban station, Boracay. Hundreds of thousands of these lightly powered bikes and sidecar taxis cruise the highways and byways of the Philippines looking for clients; turn and stop signals optional!

Three hundred years in the convent, fifty years in
Hollywood – Old Philippine adage
(repeated in Michael Palin's *Full Circle*, 1997)

The Philippines is unique amongst its neighbours.
A devoutly Christian country, it has melded
conservative 'Old World' influences with 'New
World' trends, without losing its most ancient
traditions.

   The phrase 'the sum of its parts' could well
have been invented to describe the culture here.
Just like the bulbs of garlic that grow in abundance, you can pull apart each 'clove' and discov-
er more about how it contributes to the whole.

   Life has been hard for most and still is for
many, but Filipinos are known for their
resilience. What may be more of a surprise is the
palpable *joie de vivre* that's apparent wherever
you travel. Exuberance and openness are national
characteristics, which helps to ensure that
Filipino culture is diverse, energetic and evolving.

Left: *This magnificent Taoist temple in Cebu
City is testament to the influence that Chinese
immigrants and settlers have had on modern
Filipino society.*

Historical Timeline
Aeons Ago – the Filipino Racial Mix

There has been settlement on the Philippines since the earliest time of hominids. Fragments of stone tools found in the Cagayan Valley in the north of Luzon indicate that the first Filipinos were related to *Homo erectus*, who was also making a home in China and Indonesia at the same time, around 750,000 years ago. *Homo sapiens* were making a living on Palawan 47,000 years ago. Tabon Caves at Lipuun Point in the middle of Palawan show evidence of continual habitation over several generations.

There are many other remains at the Tabon Caves, dating from after the last Ice Age when sea levels rose and changed the topography into the myriad islands we see today. The first migratory settlers arrived from the east. These were the first subsistence farmers who used the caves on Lipuun Point on Palawan for their burial rituals. These Negrito peoples are thought to have reached the Philippines from around the Southeast Asian region but there's still a lot to learn about their lifestyle. Around 8000BC settlers from Indonesia intermingled with the Negritos and they were joined by the Austronesian peoples, migrating southwards from Taiwan and southern China, who settled in the Philippines and then later spread out east and west to form both the Polynesians and the Malays.

Right: You won't have to look too hard to find a smile; Filipinos are naturally exuberant and love to have a good time.

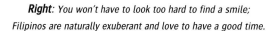

c45,000BC	c10,000BC	c8000BC	c6000BC	c900AD	c1200AD
Early Homo sapiens settle the caves around Lipuun Point on Palawan.	After the end of the last Ice Age the Negrito peoples settle across the islands.	Another wave of settlers from Indonesia arrive from the southwest.	The Negritos were joined by the Austronesian peoples, migrating southwards from Taiwan and southern China, settling in the Philippines and later spreading out east and west to form both the Polynesians and the Malays.	Trade routes are well established with the Chinese to the north and with what is now Indonesia to the southwest.	Islam filters across the Sulu Sea from the Indonesian archipelago to the Philippine islands.

1450	1521	27 April 1521	1565	1570
Abu Bakr founds the Sulu Sultanate, the first of a series of Islamic fiefdoms that cements the Islamic faith in the south.	Ferdinand Magellan lands on Suluan as part of his quest to find a trade route to China for the Spanish, to herald the arrival of Europeans. On 31 March 1521 the first Christian mass is held for Magellan's men.	Magellan is killed by local leader Lapu-Lapu.	Miguel Lopez de Legazpi arrives with a second Spanish expedition, founding a settlement at Cebu.	Martin de Goiti is sent by Legazpi to explore 'Maynilad' to the north. Goiti engages the local leader Rajah Soliman and the latter's fort is destroyed.

Early Trading Links

By the end of the first millennium AD the peoples were thriving due to a well-established farming industry and lucrative trade links with the Malay archipelago and with China. The wreck of a Chinese trading ship that sank fully loaded and was found off Puerto Galera in Mindanao suggests that trade was sophisticated, with goods pre-packaged for particular clients rather than simply loaded for sale at the port.

Founding of the Islamic Sultanates

The first Islamic burials found on the islands date back to the mid-12th century. Arab trader Abu Bakr is popularly credited with introducing the religion to the Philippines. He landed in the region in 1450 and eventually created a powerful sultanate incorporating the islands of the southern Philippines and areas of what are now Indonesia and Malaysia. The religion grew in strength as more contacts were made with Islamic Borneo (now part of Indonesia) to the southwest, but it never reached Luzon.

Europeans Make Landfall

Ferdinand Magellan landed in 1521 at Suluan, south of Samar, to herald contact with Europe. The Magellan expedition was a blatantly commercial venture funded by King Charles of Spain (though Magellan himself was Portuguese) to access the treasures of the east. After 18 months at sea, they

1571	c1570	1574	1603	1762	1815
Legazpi founds Fort Santiago on the ruins of the Rajah's fort, around which the city of Intramuros (Manila) becomes capital of the new Spanish colony of Las Filipinas, ruled from the colony in Mexico.	The 'Manila galleon' trade begins, carrying spices and Chinese ceramics to Mexico with silver returning to Las Filipinas.	Intramuros is attacked by Limahong, a Chinese pirate.	The itinerant Chinese workforce rebels against the Spanish. They are banished from Intramuros and establish the Parian district outside the walls.	The British take Las Filipinas during the Seven Year War, withdrawing in 1764.	The galleon trade ends with devastating effects on the economy.

Statistics

Total number of islands in the archipelago: 7107

Number of inhabited islands: c4000

Territorial waters: 2,200,000km² (849,200 sq miles)

Land area: 299,000km² (115,414 sq miles)

Capital: Manila

Highest point: Mount Apo on Mindanao, 2954m (9692ft)

Population: 88 million (2007 estimate)

Religions: 90% Christian (80% Catholic), 8% Muslim, with animist, Taoist and Buddhist adherents

Official language: Two languages: Pilipino, based heavily on the tribal dialect Tagalog, and English

Government: A democratic state with a governmental system based on that of the United States of America

President: Gloria Macapagal-Arroyo (since 2001)

Currency: The national currency is the Philippine peso (PHP). Each peso is made up of 100 centavos.

Time: The Philippines is 8 hours ahead of Greenwich Mean Time.

Literacy rates: 94%

Life expectancy: 69 (67 for men and 72 for women)

Population living below the poverty line: 40%

were dishevelled and starving. Local leader Rajah Kolambu met with them and they celebrated the first Catholic mass on Philippine soil on 31 March.

Battle of Mactan

Magellan was directed to Cebu where he was asked to pay tribute to the ruler Rajah Humabon. Magellan refused because he said his King was so powerful that he didn't need to pay tribute. He did, however, exchange gifts with

Left: Lapu-Lapu was the tribal leader who struck down and killed explorer Ferdinand Magellan during a battle on Mactan Island in 1521, but this incident didn't stop European interest in the area, and Miguel Legazpi claimed the islands for the Spanish Crown in 1565.

the ruler. Humabon was persuaded to accept the protection of the Spanish throne and to embrace Christianity (the Santo Niño statue is Magellan's baptismal gift), after which other local tribal leaders began to be pressured to follow suit. Lapu-Lapu, leader of Mactan Island, refused and on 27 April Magellan was forced to confront him for the honour of his new ally and the Spanish crown. The Spanish forces were outnumbered almost 20 to 1 and in the ensuing skirmish Lapu-Lapu killed Magellan.

Legazpi and the Founding of a Colony

One ship from Magellan's expedition fled back to Spain where, despite the dramatic tales, the cargo of spices still sparked interest amongst merchants and adventurers who wanted to emulate Magellan. Ruy Lopez de

1821	1896	12 November 1897	25 April 1898	1 May 1898
When Mexico gains independence, Las Filipinas falls under direct rule from Spain for the first time.	The Spanish authorities discover a secret society, the Kapitunan, whose aim is to create an independent Las Filipinas. They round up prominent citizens in an attempt to quash the organization. On 30 December leading writer Jose Rizal is shot for treason.	Leaders of the revolution announce the founding of a Filipino Republic headed by Emilio Aguinaldo, but this is not recognized internationally.	America declares war on Spain over problems in Cuba.	American naval vessels attack the Spanish fleet in Manila Harbour.

12 June 1898	25 July 1898	13 August 1898	29 September 1898	19 December 1898
Filipinos declare independence from Spain a second time.	American forces persuade the Filipino troops to move aside and let them attack Intramuros (Manila).	Spanish forces surrender to the Americans.	A third declaration of independence by the Filipinos meets with no international recognition.	As part of the Treaty of Paris, Spain sells Las Filipinas to the United States of America (along with Guam and Puerto Rico) for US$20 million, becoming the Philippines.

Villalobos named the islands Las Filipinas during his expedition but died during spats with the Portuguese, who also liked the look of the place. Finally, Miguel Lopez de Legazpi arrived in 1565.

Legazpi ended up on Bohol when his boat hit bad weather as he tried to make it to Mindanao. They met with a bad reception. The Boholeños had already been scammed by a group of Portuguese adventurers posing as agents of the Spanish crown and were twice shy about more Europeans. However, Legazpi did negotiate a blood compact between himself and the Rajah Sikatuna, one of their chieftains. The Spanish moved on to Cebu where, after a fierce battle, the defeated Rajah Tupas signed all Filipinos into the hands of the Spanish and the Catholic Church.

In 1570, Legazpi sent Martin de Goiti to lay the groundwork in 'Maynilad' (Tagalog for 'the place where the mangrove grows') to the north. The local leader Rajah Soliman was considered the most powerful chief in the region, with influence over others. During negotiations, a rogue cannonball was shot from the Spanish galleon and in the ensuing fracas the Rajah's fort was destroyed. The Spanish took control of the Rajah's lands, including its native Filipinos and a large contingent of Chinese traders who were well ensconced. The Spanish began to build Fort Santiago and the walled town of Intramuros, the new capital of their colony Las Filipinas.

The Early Days

The fledgling colony was put under the control of the Spanish regime in Mexico, across the Pacific, and within a very short space of time a profitable sea route linked Mexico, Manila and China, bringing the best goods from each country. The 'Manila galleons', as the ships were known, brought great wealth

Left: Miguel Legazpi landed on Bohol in 1565 with the express intent of expanding the already vast Spanish empire. His first negotiations resulted in a 'blood pact' between himself and local tribal lord Sikatuna, to signify a close accord between the two, and commemorated in this fine bronze diorama.

January 1899	4 February 1899	1 April 1901	4 July 1902	1907	1916
The new Filipino regime issues a constitution.	The Philippine-American War begins.	Aguinaldo pledges allegiance to the American regime.	The Philippine-American War is declared over.	A Philippine National Assembly is inaugurated.	The Philippine Autonomy Act passed in the US promises withdrawal as soon as stable government is established.

to the colony. Silver from Mexico started a new fashion in the Philippines, while silk, ivory, pearls and shells loaded in Manila were all the rage in Acapulco.

The Spanish faced their first serious threat in 1574 when they were attacked by Limahong, a Chinese pirate with a huge fleet and a force of around 3000 men. Manila was spared by the surprise return of part of Legazpi's fleet, which had been out surveying the Ilocos coastline to the north.

Later, the Chinese king sent a delegation to bring back famed gold from northern Luzon. This didn't actually exist, as they discovered when they arrived, but the Spanish were suspicious and upped security measures against a possible Chinese invasion. The Chinese community in Manila felt suppressed and eventually rebelled in 1603. Twenty thousand Chinese were killed according to Spanish chronicles. However, after the massacre the Spanish still encouraged Chinese settlers because they needed the labour. In Manila they were ordered to live outside the walls of Intramuros in an area called the Parian. Parians grew up in all the major colonial cities.

The Undefeated South

In the early 1700s, though well established in the northern islands, the Spanish had been unable to bring Mindanao and the southern Islamic Sultanates under their control. Muslim raiders attacked Christian settlements and the *Moros*, as the Spanish called the Muslims, were a constant thorn in their side. In one incident, the Battle of Lamintan in 1637, the Spanish defeated the forces of Sultan Kudarat, but he escaped to regroup and pull in other anti-Spanish factions.

In the end the Spanish never held control in these regions, just as they never defeated the tribes of the Cordillera in northern Luzon. These mountain people were very much left to their own devices, which is one reason why they still have their rich traditional customs and practices today.

The Brits Cometh

When the Seven Year War (1756–63) between Britain and France started, Spain allied itself to France but news of the alliance had not yet reached the Philippines when a fleet of British ships arrived in Manila Bay. The Spanish assumed they were trading ships and 3000 troops had disembarked before the penny dropped. The British took the city with ease; however, the greater colony stayed loyal to Spain. When news of the end of the war reached the British contingent in 1764, they withdrew without question – though they took a ransom of treasures and cash.

Economic and Political Changes

The galleon trade finally came to an end with Mexican independence. The Philippines lost lucrative income and had to cut ties with the Mexicans, a people it had worked closely with for almost 300 years. The colony fell under direct rule by Spain in 1821 and all trade had to go through Madrid. But by 1854 it was clear that the colony could not survive on the money earned from ties with Spain alone, and the

1934	1935	11 December 1941	24 December 1941	2 January 1942	6 May 1942
The Tydings-McDuffie Act sets a 10-year timetable for Philippine independence.	Manuel L Quezon is elected Philippine President. He is re-elected in 1940.	The Japanese decimate the American fleet at Pearl Harbor and begin their assault on Southeast Asia.	Quezon and the government are evacuated from Manila.	Japanese troops enter Manila.	The Philippines is in Japanese hands.

Philippines opened up to foreign trade. This resulted in an expansion of commercial districts in every town – and a whole new wave of foreign arrivals.

A Tide of Nationalism

Spain's standing in the world continued to decline as the century progressed, and in the years after Mexican independence many Filipinos began harbouring dreams about their own country's future. The Spanish, of course, refused to relinquish any control, so an underground movement developed, helped by men like writer and social philosopher Jose Rizal who travelled extensively and gained an international perspective on the problem.

The Kataastaasan Kagalanggalang Katipunan ng mga Anak ng Bayan (meaning Highest and Most Venerable Association of Sons and Daughters of the Nation), often shortened to Katipunan, was a secret society of Filipinos in all strata of society working towards liberty for the country. Membership rose from a mere few hundred in 1892 to over 30,000 by 1895. It was exposed in 1896, following which Spanish authorities went on a witch hunt and arrested several hundred prominent citizens, including powerful mestizo (mixed Spanish/Filipino or Spanish/Chinese blood) movers and shakers. Support for the Spanish began to wane.

Jose Rizal was inspiring the nation with his books, highlighting the situation in the Philippines, but he incurred the wrath of the Spanish. Arrested in 1896, he was sentenced to death and shot on 30 December. Today he is a national hero.

An uprising swiftly followed the shocking events. This was quelled in Manila where the Spanish were at their strongest but gained momentum in other parts of the colony. On 12 November 1897, leaders of the revolutionary movement announced the founding of a republic from their stronghold at Biak-na-Bato, San Miguel, in Bulacan, but it couldn't garner support abroad and didn't have the momentum at home to carry its quest through. Likewise, the Spanish couldn't summon the forces to destroy the revolutionary movement. Rebel leader Emilio Aguinaldo and the Spanish army's Miguel Primo de Rivera met to discuss proposals for a truce, but the agreement didn't last.

1898 – The Almost Year

By 1898 Spanish power worldwide had dwindled. It had lost many of its New World colonies and the associated lucrative trade revenues. When revolution was sparked in Cuba, Spain had the misfortune to incur the wrath of the USA when the battleship *Maine* was sunk under mysterious circumstances in Havana harbour. America declared war on 25 April. The Spanish fleet in Manila Bay – though old and decrepit – was a prime target for the Americans. A fleet under Admiral Dewey did the job in a few hours on the morning of 1 May.

On 12 June 1898 a declaration of Philippine independence was written and proclaimed at Aguinaldo's home, but the Spanish were still installed at Intramuros. The USA had not officially recognized this proclamation and the American fleet was stationed in Manila Bay. Filipino forces surrounded the capital,

20 October 1944	February 1945	4 July 1946	1965	1969
General MacArthur lands on Philippine soil to begin the recapture of the islands.	Over 90% of Manila is destroyed and 150,000 civilians lose their lives in fierce fighting between allied and Japanese troops. By June 1945 Japanese resistance is ended.	The Philippines becomes a republic (Republika ng Pilipinas) with Manuel Roxas as first president.	Ferdinand Marcos is elected president and begins a programme of reform and reinvestment. The Vietnam War means the US relies on Philippine support and they cultivate the regime.	Marcos is re-elected but economic progress is not maintained. Political opposition begins to grow and this turns into violence.

sensing the death knell of the old regime.

On 25 July, General Anderson, in charge of American ground troops attacking the capital, was successful in persuading Aguinaldo to move his troops aside to allow an American assault on Intramuros. The Filipinos were entreated to 'trust the good will and sense of justice of the American people.' The Spanish, reassured by this move, surrendered to the Americans on 13 August. No Filipinos were present at the surrender, nor was the fledgling state mentioned in the surrender document.

On 15 September a Filipino congress met in Malolos, Bulacan province, which resulted in another declaration of independence on 29 September. It garnered not a jot of international support.

Meanwhile, the Spanish and Americans were in negotiations on a peace deal. The Treaty of Paris signed on 19 December saw the Philippines sold to the United States for $20 million. This didn't sit well with everyone in the United States congress – the treaty was ratified by a single vote over the minimum needed – but nonetheless, it was ratified. President McKinley stated that the territory was to undergo 'benevolent assimilation by friends not invaders.'

The Philippine-American War

Meanwhile, back in the Philippines, a constitution was proclaimed in January 1899 and Aguinaldo was installed as president. There was an unstoppable momentum for self-determination so the Philippine-American War began on 4 February 1899. Tactics employed by the Americans included conducting accords with the *Moro* sultans

21 September 1972	17 January 1981	21 August 1983	February 1986	25 February 1986
Close to the end of his second and final term, Marcos declares martial law.	Marcos lifts martial law. He wins a June election with 88% of the vote.	Benigno Aquino, political opponent of Marcos, is shot dead within minutes of returning from political exile. The Marcos regime is suspected.	Marcos calls a snap election and Aquino's widow Corazon stands against him. Marcos is declared the winner but the result brings mass protests around the country. When the EDSA highway in Manila comes to a standstill due to the crowds, the military withdraw their support for Marcos and he flees to Hawaii on the 25th.	Corazon Aquino is declared president of the Philippines.

against the Filipinos, but they were desperate to capture Aguinaldo who was acting both as political and military head of his people and thus the fulcrum of the independence movement. He was tricked into surrender when Tagalog-speaking Macabebes allied to the Americans played the part of revolutionaries sent to reinforce his garrison. Aguinaldo pledged allegiance to America in a declaration on 1 April 1901 and the revolutionary movement lost its momentum, though the war was not officially declared over until 4 July 1902. The intervening 15 months brought massacres and bloody reprisals.

The American Regime

There were also voices of concern in the USA about the morality of US 'colonization'. In 1907, a Philippine National Assembly was formed to offer a semblance of self-rule, and in the 1916 Philippine Autonomy Act the USA resolved to withdraw from the country 'as soon as stable government can be established', but throughout the 1920s this was never seriously discussed. Then in 1934 the US Tydings-McDuffie Act set a 10-year timetable for Philippine independence. In 1935, elections in the Philippines voted Manuel L Quezon into the presidency with Sergio Osmeña as his deputy. The countdown to independence had begun.

Left: The monumental central edifice of the War Memorial at the American Cemetery on the outskirts of Manila houses a small chapel, where a candle burns to remember those who lost their lives in battles during the fierce fighting of World War II.

The Second World War

On 11 December 1941 the devastating Japanese attack on the US fleet at Pearl Harbor rendered much of the Pacific defenceless and imperial forces swept across the region. On 24 December, Quezon and the government were evacuated and General MacArthur, head of the defending forces, declared Manila an open city to save the civilian population. Japanese ground forces arrived on 2 January 1942. Filipino/American forces in the rest of the country surrendered on 9 April and the last American forces dug in on the Bataan Peninsula surrendered on 6 May. MacArthur too was evacuated but vowed to return. However, the Philippines was now in Japanese hands.

After America turned the Japanese tide in the Pacific, a series of gruelling, bloody battles ensued.

MacArthur returned on 20 October 1944, landing on Leyte with President Osmeña (Quezon having died in exile), but the Japanese weren't about to give the Philippines up without a fight. The Battle of Manila that took place over February 1945 saw the bloodiest and most destructive fighting. It's estimated that at least 150,000 Filipino citizens died, and the city was reduced to rubble.

Those with an interest in the battles of World War II should visit the American War Cemetery (specifically the War Memorial) on the outskirts of Manila, where a series of huge mosaic tableaux show the locations of major movements in the lead-up to the Japanese expulsion from the Philippines.

June 1991	1992	1998	2001	20 January 2001	2004
Mount Pinatubo blows its top in the second most powerful volcanic eruption of the 20th century.	Aquino steps down after one administration and Fidel Ramos wins the election.	Actor Joseph Estrada wins the Presidential election.	Estrada is implicated in a racketeering ring and is driven from power by mass protests known as EDSA II. When the army turned against him, Estrada was replaced. He was placed under house arrest in 2000 and after a long trial was found guilty of embezzlement and sentenced to life in prison in September 2007.	Estrada's Vice-President, Gloria Macapagal-Arroyo, is sworn into power.	Arroyo wins another term in office.

And, At Last, Independence

In the immediate aftermath of the war, the Philippines had to take stock of the massive cost of the battle for liberation. Reconstruction began in earnest, as did the rebuilding of the political fabric. On 4 July 1946 the country became officially independent, with newly elected Manuel Roxas as first president.

The Marcos Regime

Meanwhile, a young lawyer, Ferdinand Marcos, was rising through the political ranks, entering the House of Representatives in 1949. In 1965 he was elected president on a promise of putting right a country in financial crisis.

The Marcos era coincided with the Vietnam War, when the Philippines became a vital ally to the Americans and a physical stepping-stone for men and materials. Marcos ploughed resources into much-needed public works and the economy began to expand rapidly. Patronage of the arts, mostly by the first lady, saw Manila life flourish and take on a higher global profile. Marcos easily won a second term but then problems began to surface. Anti-war factions and the Muslim separatist movement both found coherent voices and social unrest grew. Marcos was approaching the end of his second term and he knew he could not stand again, so to keep a hold on power, he declared martial law in 1972. The republican constitution was torn up and a new one gave Marcos absolute power. Opposition politicians, including Benigno Aquino, were arrested. Marcos controlled all economic activities in the Philippines, taking massive payoffs on commercial deals. The benefits of economic reform stopped trickling down through the social system, but Marcos and his coterie became super-rich.

Right: The Philippine national flag was designed by Emilio Aguinaldo. In the centre of the white triangle representing equality and fraternity is a sun with eight rays representing the eight provinces. The blue stands for peace while the red is for patriotism and bravery.

The Downfall of Marcos

Throughout the 1970s opposition to Marcos began to grow. The Catholic Church took up the cause, while hopes for the political future centred on Aquino, who was by now in exile in the United States. Marcos lifted martial law in 1981 but fixed the presidential election. In 1983, Aquino decided to return to the Philippines to restart political opposition. He was shot through the head at the airport within minutes of landing in Manila; evidence pointed to the Marcos regime.

The opposition immediately put their support behind Aquino's widow, Corazon, who was backed in turn by leading cleric Cardinal Sin. It was a groundswell even Marcos could not ignore. He called a quick election in February 1986 to snuff out the threat but Corazon Aquino took the gauntlet and announced that she would run against his corrupt regime. Both candidates claimed victory, but while the National Assembly recognized Marcos as president, an independent election watchdog reported widespread irregularities in the voting. Voices of dissent were growing into a wave that spread throughout the country, and on 22 February key members of the Marcos regime finally began to turn against him. Thousands of Filipinos blockaded Epifanio de los Santos (EDSA) Boulevard between the city's main military bases and the troops stood aside and let the protests continue. Power was ebbing away from Marcos. On 25 February, Marcos was inaugurated president but it was a hollow event. He fled the Philippines that day for Hawaii. Aquino became president, inheriting a $27-billion debt, while the country's neighbouring 'tiger economies' were experiencing unprecedented economic growth.

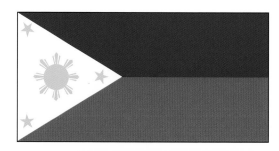

Post Marcos

Although Aquino had a massive mandate through the EDSA movement (as the anti-Marcos protests became known), taking on the problems left behind by the Marcos regime was an almost impossible task. She had to galvanize the disparate opposition groups, curb corruption and kick-start the economy. There were several *coup* attempts during her regime, all backed by the military. A whole raft of reforms was introduced but many foundered in the quagmire of endemic corruption and economic stagnation. Even so, for her courageous stand, Corazon Aquino won the 1986 *Time* Woman of the Year Award and was nominated for the Nobel Peace Prize.

In June 1991, the massive problems of the economy were overshadowed by natural disaster when Mount Pinatubo blew its top, killing hundreds of people and leaving many thousands homeless.

Aquino didn't stand for a second term and backed Fidel Ramos, a military man, for the job. Ramos won but didn't have a strong mandate, garnering only 24% of the vote. One significant event during the Ramos administration took place in 1996 when areas of Moro Mindanao were granted a certain amount of self-rule under the title Autonomous Region of Muslim Mindanao (comprising Tawi Tawi, Sulu, Maguindanao and Lanao del Sur).

The 1998 election had a more convincing result. It was won by Joseph Estrada, a popular actor. But things started to go wrong for Estrada from the outset. The Moro Islamic Liberation Front started a violent campaign for total independence of the southern Muslim states with a series of bombings, and the fragile economy finally stalled. Estrada was implicated in a gambling racket, and although he tried to hang on to power, the people took to the streets again to voice their opinion, a movement that became known as EDSA II. When the army turned against him, Estrada was replaced. He was placed under house arrest in 2000, and after a long trial was found guilty of embezzlement and sentenced to life in prison in September 2007, but walked free in October of the same year after being granted a full presidential pardon.

The Third Millennium

Estrada's vice-president, Gloria Macapagal-Arroyo, took office and has been serving ever since. She won the 2004 election and ironically her main rival for the post was another Filipino actor, Fernando Poe. Once again, however, the scent of corruption dogged the office of the president after Arroyo was caught on tape ordering an aide to 'fix' the election. Although she denies corruption, she has admitted the voice on the recording is hers, and that the call was an 'error in judgement'.

Arroyo has also had to contend with increased terrorist action by Muslim separatists, including bombings in Manila. In February 2006 another alleged *coup d'état* was foiled and Arroyo declared a state of emergency (lifted on 3 March). A number of leftist politicians were charged after widespread protests broke out. Continued crackdowns on Arroyo critics have drawn protests from around the Filipino diaspora. The jury is still out on her continued rule.

Culture
The Contribution of the Cross

The overriding legacy of the Spanish is Roman Catholicism. This is the only staunchly Christian country in this part of Southeast Asia and it's had a major influence on the culture. Through all the trials and tribulations in Philippine history, and in the daily lives of Filipinos, the church has been one constant. In the modern era it has remained centre stage, sustaining the population after the Mount Pinatubo eruption and inciting opposition to the Marcos regime. Everyone attends Mass on a Sunday morning and there's a fervent show of faith during all Christian festivals.

Statues have become beacons of hope and several have been imbued with miraculous powers. Devotion to the Virgin Mary is a major component in Catholic worship but Santo Niño, the Christ Child, is specifically Filipino. Santo Niño was the original lucky emblem given to Magellan by the Queen of Spain to protect him during his journey of discovery.

When he landed in the Philippines, Magellan gifted the statue to the Cebueños (inhabitants of Cebu) following the first Mass under the wooden cross he erected in 1521, and it was found again by Legazpi almost 50 years later lying miraculously undamaged in a burnt-out *nipa* hut after a battle between the Cebueños and the Spanish. Today, the statue is dressed in gem-encrusted garments in its alter at the Basilica Minore in Cebu City.

Other Santo Niños can now be found around the islands, and the Feast of Santo Niño brings hundreds of thousands out onto the streets on the third Sunday in January.

Santo Niño was the patron saint of the Philippines but has recently been replaced by his mother in the guise of Our Lady of Guadeloupe. The Vatican insists that patron saint status is reserved for humans who have transcended into grace, where the Christ Child lived a life in grace and was therefore ineligible. However, the Vatican missive doesn't stop effigies of the statue from being sold outside all the major churches in the country, from dashboard size for jeepney drivers to double actual size and larger.

Another miraculous statue is the Black Nazarene at Quiapo, Manila. Carved in Mexico by an Aztec artisan

and transported to the Philippines in 1606, a Papal Bull in 1650 granted indulgence (remission of time in purgatory) to all those who prayed here. This has ensured a throng of devotees to the present day and the city comes to a standstill when the statue is paraded through the streets on 9 January.

For all the influence that the Catholic Church exerts in the Philippines, one thing you'll notice is how careworn many of the buildings are, with ceilings damaged by water ingress and mould on the walls. Any shiny new churches you see on your travels are sure to belong to the Filipino Independent Church or Iglesia ni Cristo, a church based on Unitarianism and founded by Felix Manalo in 1914 with himself as God's prophet.

Secular Society

Though the Spanish claimed much Philippine soil as their sovereign territory, they were few in number and set up power bases in certain enclaves. Fort San Pedro in Cebu City was the first colonial stone building started in 1565, and indeed, Cebu was the first capital until Legazpi decamped to Manila, so it can claim to be the birthplace of the Philippines.

Fort Santiago in Manila was the second and much larger fort built by Legazpi in 1571, but this in turn was surrounded by a more substantial fortification, Intramuros ('within the walls'), a true city where the religious and secular authorities of Las Filipinas had their headquarters. It was from Intramuros that the Chinese were banned after their uprising in 1603, after which the Chinese-dominated Parian district grew up just outside the walls. Both these fortifications served through the Spanish-American War and the American-Filipino War and were used in World War II by both the Americans and Japanese.

What's in a Name?

Why is the country name spelled the Philippines when the people are internationally known as Filipino, and why do they call themselves Pilipino? In many ways the answer to this question ties together the major strands of Philippine identity and history.

The spelling is simple. The first Spanish colonialists named the islands Las Filipinas after the then king of Spain, Felipe II. The local people couldn't pronounce Filipinas because there is no 'f' sound in the native Tagalog dialect, so called the country Las Pilipinas and themselves Pilipino. Finally, the spelling was anglicized to the Philippines when the Americans arrived.

Right: The ornate altar of the Basilica Minore del Santo Niño in Cebu City signifies the power of Catholicism in Filipino society. For centuries Santo Niño was the patron saint of the country and the miraculous statue is still revered by the population.

Latin Expansion

Over time more families of Spanish and Spanish/ Mexican stock came and settled in the Philippines, but to farm and trade rather than to conquer and defend. Vigan in the north was built on the profits of plantation farming, while Iloilo became home to several plantation-owning families who then spread out to secondary sites on Bohol, Negros Occidental and Negros Oriental. The influence of the homeland stayed strong with these families through the generations – some even now speak Spanish at home – and they maintained a link with the mainstream arts scene in Europe. Painting, poetry, and the playing of musical instruments were normal pastimes for the cultured. But compared to their colonies in the New World, the number of Spanish settlers was few; they were far outnumbered by the Chinese for instance.

The Spanish combined European styles of architecture with practical native *nipa* hut design that became 'mode Las Filipinas'. The lower floors of their mansions were constructed of stone, usually the common coral stone, with a hardwood upper floor. Goods were stored downstairs while the family lived on the upper floor. Glass was impossible to come by, so thin layers of *capiz* shell were inserted into wooden sliding frames to act as windows. These could be opened fully to allow cooling breezes to play through the house. Hardwood gingerbread decoration gussied up the outside and *santos*, or statues of the saints, were part of the interior decoration.

The Architectural Legacy

The mestizo district of Vigan is the most complete example of period architecture, especially the mansions along Callé Crisologo, rendered all the more authentic by the horse-drawn *calesas* that trot along the streets. There are tantalizing glimpses of the gen-

Left: Fort San Pedro in Cebu City was the site of the first Spanish settlement in the Philippines, and the colony's original short-lived capital. The guns now lie silent, but the fort saw service as recently as World War II.

teel life of the Spanish settlers at Casa Manila in Intramuros, a reconstructed house with genuine items taken from period homes that once stood in Intramuros. Other mansions include Clarin Ancestral Home at Loay and Casa Rocha-Suarez Heritage Center at Tagbilaran, both on Bohol; Casa Gorordo built circa 1863 in Cebu City, and Ylagen de la Rosa Ancestral home at Taal City in south Luzon. Taal has streets flanked by a collection of historic houses but many are in a poor state of repair. Sitio Remedios is an unusual hotel where you'll spend your stay in one of a dozen renovated traditional houses.

The Original Filipinos

The indigenous peoples of the Philippines number over six million, with around 40 different tribes or groups. Though not different in ethnic origin from other Filipinos, their remote homes in the mountains of northern Luzon and in Mindanao/Zamboanga in the south helped cement their cultural identity even before the arrival of the Catholic and Islamic influences. After colonization they were further isolated from the lowland Filipinos, thus preserving their beliefs and traditions into the modern age. Though some attempts at integration were made during the American administration, the lifestyles of the indigenous peoples are still a rich reference for scholars and a source of fascination for travellers. Though each individual tribe has a name and a dialect, scientists have grouped the northern Cordillera native groups under the name Igorot and the southern tribes as Manobo.

The Cordillera

All the indigenous mountain peoples are agrarian with a principal crop of rice. The famed rice terraces of northern Luzon, created by the Ifugao Igorots, were begun as early as 1150BC to increase the arable surface of the steep slopes, and have been in use since then, carefully maintained through the centuries. Most of these peoples have animist beliefs, with elaborate rituals connected with the rice harvest and protection of their crops. Anthropologists

Previous page: *A traditional* calesa *plies its route past the magnificent Spanish mansions on Calle Crisologo in the historic heart of Vigan.*
Below: *An Ifugao tribal elder in traditional costume, displaying the colourful textiles that form an important part of the culture.*

have identified over 100 god and nature deities but the *bulul*, or rice god, is the most important. *Bulul* effigies protect the rice in the fields and in the granaries, and their spirits are appeased by regular sacrifices, most often goats or pigs, but also rice wine and rice cakes. Wealth is measured by the size of rice-growing areas,

livestock, family heirlooms, textiles and beads.

To enter the world of the Igorot, visit the Cordillera north of Baguio and around the towns of Bontoc, Banaue and Benguet. Just remember that these are not museums or special attractions for tourists but living, breathing settlements. Note that in the more remote regions of the Cordillera, notably Kalinga country and beyond, local tribal feuds can still reignite, disrupting daily life and travel. Check with the authorities before venturing beyond the area mentioned above. The Tam-Awan Village in Baguio is a recreated Igorot village where you'll be able to explore the traditions of the people or stay the night in a native hut.

Mindanao

In contrast to the Igorots, the Manobo T'boli peoples of Lake Sebu in the south of Mindanao live by 'slash-and-burn' farming methods whereby every few years a new piece of ground is cleared of natural vegetation and the old land abandoned to nature. The T'boli carry their wealth in the form of ornate jewellery; women normally wear several earrings in each ear.

The Light of the Crescent Moon

Islam arrived in the Philippines from the south through what is now Indonesia to the islands of the Sulu Sea. Makhdum Karim is noted as the first Islamic scholar to spread the word, though Arab trader Abu Bakr is credited with introducing the religion to the Philippines.

Abu Bakr's well-ordered fiefdom ensured that Islam was well integrated into all aspects of life. It spread across the southern Philippine islands, though it made little inroad in Luzon. Those not converted moved to the hills to continue their animist lifestyles. Palawan had originally been part of the sultanate but was ceded to the Spanish in 1705, after which a programme of Catholicization changed the religious character of the island.

Moro Resistance

The Moros, as the Spanish called the Islamic converts, were not one united people but many different indige-

nous tribal groups. Some were farmers, while others looked to the sea, being fishermen or, more fascinatingly, pirates, undertaking raiding parties to capture slaves and booty. The Spanish tried to quash this practice, but it was only under the Americans that real attempts were made when the sultanates were broken and settlers from the north took Muslim land. Vast plantations were founded around the new city of General Santos during the 1930s on Moro land. During this time the first organized Islamic resistance movements were formed, the precursors of today's independence fighters, the Moro Islamic Liberation Front and Abu Sayyaf, a particularly militant group said to have perpetrated the rash of bombings in the country since 2000. Some have theorized that the continued piracy in the South China Sea is simply Moro tradition for a new purpose; to fund their freedom campaigns.

Today, in western Mindanao and the small islands of the Sulu Sea, the minarets of mosques take the place of the church spires of the north, and the lilting cry of the muezzin punctuates the day at prayer time. The Mosque of Sheik Makhdum on Simunul Island, named after the founding scholar, is the oldest in the country and has carved posts dating from the 14th century. There is also a beautiful early mosque on the banks of Lake Lanao.

Enter the Dragon

Chinese Filipinos make up around 12% of the total population, quite a sizeable community, due firstly to the large number of Chinese citizens who settled in the country when the Spanish needed labour, and secondly to the fact that the Chinese quickly intermarried with Spanish and Filipinos and many also converted to Catholicism, cutting ties to their old homeland. They remained in the urban centres, with the largest numbers being found in Manila and Cebu. Spanish/Chinese mestizo (mixed blood) families dominate trade and land ownership and have made a great contribution to the oligarchic system that some say still holds the reins of power in the country.

It's interesting to note that beautiful Chinese Taoist and Buddhist temples in the major centres of population cater mainly to the recently arrived Chinese. Visit the Bell Church in Baguio to see a fusion of styles. The Temple of the 9th Heaven in Cebu City is the largest such complex in the country.

Hollywood Comes to Town

The parting gift of the Americans was democracy – and it's been an interesting ride politically since then, with a system stymied by corruption and cronyism, plus a couple of periods of martial law – but their most enduring legacy is the importance of English to the Filipinos. The physical evidence of American tenure is scant. In 1946 they didn't even leave behind a functioning capital city. Manila was a pile of rubble that many say has never been fixed.

But 40 years of American rule have left a little slice of 'apple pie' in the middle of Southeast Asia. Urban Filipinos have few qualms about diving headlong into la mode American, from food to lifestyle. Advertising everywhere pushes the clean, cute and fair-skinned model of perfection and young Filipinos and Filipinas want to belong. High-factor sunscreen is very expensive for most people so women carry umbrellas for shade and many young men in open-air jobs (boatmen, cycle-taxi drivers) wear full-face masks with holes for eyes and mouth. If you come across one of these rather dramatic hooded men, don't assume they are bank robbers; they are simply trying to stay fashionable, which means light-skinned.

The Philippines Today

In many ways the Philippines is still trying to break away from an image forged during the Marcos era. Most people know about Imelda's shoes but beyond that there's seemingly little to get a handle on, which couldn't be further from the truth. The Philippines is a fascinating country to visit. Visually stunning to be sure, but beyond this there's an intriguing cultural web to be unwound, explored, and savoured. Filipinos meet you more than halfway in this quest. They are very proud of their country – despite the obvious problems – and knowledgeable about it.

Previous page: The dragon symbolizes the power of the sage, and is a potent representation of yang energy in the Taoist religion. This intricate example decorates the Bell Church in Baguio.
Right: Makati in Manila is the modern face of the Philippines; a bustling financial and business district, it has an international vibe with fashionable shopping and dining.

Urban v. Rural

Stroll along the streets in Makati, Manila, and at first glance you could be anywhere in the modern world. Urbanites go shopping in fancy malls for the designer names, they meet friends for coffee, they listen to the latest chart hits on MP3 players. Yet move out into the countryside and on to many offshore islands and it's a very different picture. A large percentage of the Philippine population lives on the land, planting by hand and using water buffalo as beasts of burden. Many families live at a subsistence level in single-room huts made from bamboo and *nipa* palm, producing much of their own food and selling the surplus for a little extra cash. Here the pace of life moves with the seasons and the harvests, and the local market is the most important event of the week.

Familiarity Means the World

Whilst 'six degrees of separation' refers to the theory that everyone is connected to everyone else on earth with connections to six or fewer other individuals, Filipinos claim 'two degrees of separation'. The movers and shakers in society are so close knit that everyone knows everyone else through family ties, schooling or work.

The Filipino Diaspora

Overseas workers pump millions of dollars back into the country's economy every year. Many of the foreign workers are Philippine women taking maid or child-care jobs in Hong Kong and the Middle East. The number of Western Union offices you see in the

Philippines is an indication of how many families are sustained by regular deliveries of cash from abroad. Of course many of these women have children of their own, looked after by sisters or grandmothers while their mothers are away.

'Filipinos Don't Wallow in what is Miserable and Ugly.' – Imelda Marcos

Despite their problems, studies have shown that Filipinos are some of the happiest people in the world (World Values Survey) and it really shows. They smile and joke, and they really like to party. They have a national 'cup half full' approach to life. *Bayanihan* is the social *esprit de corps* that infuses every family and social group. They work together to get jobs done in farming communities and they play together in their free time.

In Christian parts of the Philippines, beauty is celebrated and enjoyed – beauty pageants abound. Imelda herself was Miss Leyte in 1953. From an early age girls take part in the annual Flores de Mayo processions, dressing up and putting on make-up. It's an honour to be selected Flores de Mayo queen when in your teens.

Battle of the Sexes

Despite being expected to be demure and self-effacing, Philippine women have a great deal of power in society.

The two female presidents since 1986 are just the tip of the iceberg; women have high-powered careers in law, education, business and banking, and a high percentage of girls go on to further education.

Hiya

A unique attribute of the Filipino character, *hiya* oils the wheels of society. *Hiya* can be referred to as shame or embarrassment, and Filipinos do their damnedest to minimize this in any social interaction. Confrontation

Below: Out in the countryside, many Filipinos eke out a living from small family-owned farms, working the land with the aid of trusty water buffalos.

and anger cause *hiya* for all parties, so you'll rarely hear shouting or see altercations. Rather courtesy, good manners and a calm demeanour are the trademarks in hotels, restaurants and shops.

The downside of *hiya* is that Filipinos find it difficult to say that they don't know something or can't do something. So you may be given fictitious directions or opening hours, or be told that something will happen when in fact it never will.

Utang Na Loob

In the Philippines, if someone does a good deed for you, you are duty-bound to repay this. It's called *utang na loob* or 'debt of honour'. On a small social scale this may

mean taking a friend out to dinner in return for lending you his car. In a larger scale, Filipino politics is chock full of men and women handed jobs in administrations to repay *utang na loob*.

Jose Rizal: Father of the Nation

The Boy Genius

Born in Calamba in southern Luzon, Rizal was a talented and artistic child. He obtained his first degree at 16, then took further courses before moving on to medicine. He travelled to Spain to complete his medical studies, claiming that the Dominican tutors in the Philippines discriminated against Filipino pupils. This discrimination would be the basis of Rizal's fight for Filipino rights.

He chose to travel extensively after his studies and is said to have mastered 22 languages. His creative talents were turned to art, journalism, music, naturalism, poetry, psychology and theology, but he also worked tirelessly to engage the Filipino diaspora with relation to nationalism and social injustice within the Philippines.

Rizal is Published

In 1887, Rizal published his first novel, *Noli Me Tangere,* a satire about the abuses of the church in his home country. A sequel, *El Filibusterismo,* followed in 1891. The Spanish authorities began to keep him and his close contacts under surveillance and in 1892, when his sister was found to be carrying anti-Catholic leaflets, he was arrested and imprisoned for a short time. He went into exile in Mindanao soon afterwards and engaged in a pro-gramme of welfare schemes. When the social unrest of 1896 began after the exposure of the Katipunan, Rizal was re-arrested, subjected to a kangaroo court and sentenced to death.

A Martyr's Death

Whilst awaiting his fate in his small cell in Fort Santiago in Intramuros, he wrote a final untitled poem – later called *Mi Último Adiós* – that is considered his nationalist masterpiece. On 30 December 1896, Rizal

Above: *Jose Rizal is considered the Father of the Nation. An academic and polyglot who travelled the world, his calls for independence resulted in his death at the hands of the Spanish in 1896.*

walked out of his cell and through the gates of Intramuros to a place then called Bagumbayan Field where he was shot by the firing squad. The spirit of the man was too big for the Spanish to control, however, and he is still revered by all Filipinos.

For further information about Jose Rizal visit the Rizal Shrine in Fort Santiago, Intramuros, where Rizal was imprisoned prior to his death (artefacts include the original manuscripts of *Mi Último Adiós* and *Noli Me Tangere*); the Rizal Shrine at the family home in Calamba which holds artefacts including some belonging to Jose; or the Rizal Museum at Talisay, near Dapitan, where Rizal lived during his days of exile.

Ferdinand Marcos: Demigod and Dictator

The Early Years

Ferdinand Edralin Marcos was born into a political family in Sarrat, Ilocos Norte, in 1919. When his father's political rival was murdered in 1935, Ferdinand was charged in connection with the crime and sentenced to ten years in jail, but after completing a law degree, he successfully conducted his own appeal.

During the war, Marcos claimed to have been the heroic leader of a resistance force, a fabrication not disavowed by the American military until after he fell from grace. He worked as assistant to President Roxas in the first years after independence and won a seat in parliament in 1949, a post he held until he moved up to the Senate in 1959. In the interim, in 1954, Marcos married Imelda Romualdez after a whirlwind romance.

The Rise to Power

Marcos entered the presidential race in 1965, and he won with a landslide on an anti-corruption ticket. His first term was by many accounts a successful one. The power of the old oligarchies was reduced and companies and land redistributed amongst ordinary Filipinos. But things went sour the longer he stayed in power. The Marcoses ran a huge and expensive 'court' and lived a lavish lifestyle. Where the oligarchies had been disbanded, Marcos's cronies took their place, using the businesses as cash cows. The regime was ruthless in its dealings and vast numbers of opponents began to 'disappear.'

Decline and Fall

In the late 70s and early 80s, Marcos was untouchable but his health was failing. It's not clear how strong his control of power was over the final few years of his tenure when Imelda was 'front of house'. When the family finally left the Philippines, they carried with them $28 million in cash and almost 300 crates of belongings (when most Filipino households couldn't even fill one crate). Frozen Swiss bank accounts held $475 million and estimates of the family's hidden assets have topped $10 billion.

In 1988, Marcos was indicted in New York on charges of racketeering but died before he could stand trial.

The body of Ferdinand Marcos lies in a sombre mausoleum in the town of Batac in Ilocos Norte close to his childhood home. A small museum has photographs of the former president and some of his dress uniforms. The Marcos family home in Sannat has few remains of Ferdinand but has interesting artefacts owned by his parents and siblings.

Many of the shoes in the Marikina Shoe Museum once belonged to Imelda Marcos, some of the thousands of pairs that were found in Malacañang Palace after the family went into exile.

Statues and Monuments

Every settlement in the Philippines, no matter how small, will have some monument or statue, perhaps marking the location of a moment in history, or honouring some local hero.

The most common statue you'll see as you travel is that of Jose Rizal, the country's national hero. He stands outside many public schools, books in hand, to encourage studiousness amongst the young. At the National Shrine in Manila a bronze of Rizal stands close to the location of his martyrdom, now designated as Rizal Park. A sombre duo of soldiers guards the monument around the clock. A very extensive and poignant monument comprises the thousands of bronze footsteps set on the ground marking Rizal's final journey from his cell in Fort Santiago in Intramuros.

A sobering statue of Benigno Aquino sits at a busy intersection of Ayala Avenue in Makati. The bronze depicts Aquino restrained by two guards in the final few minutes before he was shot dead at the Manila International Airport on his return from exile in 1983. Interestingly, the Chinese community in the Philippines felt that this was an inappropriate location for such a statue. Depictions of death are bad *feng shui*, certainly not a good portent for the heart of Manila's financial district.

There's a magnificent tableau of Filipino history in the Parian in Cebu City (once the heart of old Chinatown). The Heritage of Cebu was designed by Eduardo Castrillo and completed in 2000. Magellan and Legazpi are represented, along with Loon Kilat, a general in the Spanish era; the April 1898 Cebueño uprising against the

Spanish; and representations of the Santo Niño festival held each January.

Bohol marks the spot where the blood pact between Legazpi and Datu Sikatuna took place in three different locations. A fine bronze tableau sitting atop a crest is the most beautiful of the three but the site is least favoured as genuine by scholars, necessitating the Spanish to have to climb a near vertical slope in full armour. Further north along the coast is an area of low-lying mangroves that would have proved a far better landing place for the Spanish ships, but the rather naïve

Below: The Rizal Monument has been erected close to the place where Jose Rizal, the Philippine national hero, was shot by the Spanish on 30 December 1896. The sombre edifice attracts many Filipinos who come to pay homage to the man.

plaster commemoration does not do the site justice.

The Bataan Peninsula north of Manila saw some of the bloodiest fighting of World War II. The Dambana ng Kagitingan (Shrine of Valor), inaugurated on Mount Samat in 1970, is topped by a 92m (302ft) high cross around which graphic bronze tableaux depict scenes from the fighting. There's a further commemoration of World War II on Corregidor, in the mouth of Manila Bay, where the Pacific War Memorial is topped by a symbolic metal flame.

The 'People's Revolution' that freed the country from the yoke of dictatorship is commemorated on EDSA at the corner of Quezon Avenue. Here, vast crowds gathered after the 1986 elections, bringing Manila to a standstill and sounding the death knell for the Marcos regime. 'People Power', a gigantic bronze ensemble covering over 1000m² (10,760 sq ft), composed by Eduardo

Castrillo, is backed by the Wall of Remembrance with the names of the dead and disappeared. Castrillo's most powerful image is a distraught mother holding her lifeless son, a metaphor for the sons lost by their mother country.

Music and Dance

Several different strands of music and dance from varying genres come together in the Philippines, drawing inspiration from the past and from present fashion.

Tribal Music and Dance

Music and dance are an integral element in the life of the indigenous peoples. Songs and dances mark the major events in life – birth, circumcision, baptism, the onset of menstruation, courtship, marriage, sickness and death – and also daily tasks such as planting, harvesting and fishing, where singing and dancing get everyone 'in the mood'.

War dances were especially important when preparing to do battle, and tribes involved in the practice also had elaborate rituals around head-hunting. These dances may be the stylized re-enactments of mock battles. This was both to reinforce good practice and to educate the young.

Instruments

There's a veritable orchestra of instruments in this musical world, most often simply made with natural products found locally in the region. Common instruments have different names in each of the regional dialects. However, there can be marked differences between the ensembles of northern Luzon and the ensembles of Mindanao in the south.

Below: Dance plays an important role in traditional indigenous culture, bringing communities together at harvest time, to mark a coming battle, or to celebrate a right of passage.

Wind Instruments

Flutes are fabricated from slim sections of bamboo. The standard three-hole flute is played with the lips (the *kaldong* in Kalinga or *pulalu* in Manobo), while several groups also have the nose flute (the *tongali* in Igorot). Flutes can also be put together to produce polyphone pipes or panpipes (the *diwdiw-as* in Igorot and *saggeypo* in Kalinga), with several chambers of differing lengths strapped side-by-side.

Stringed Instruments

The zither is a stringed instrument made from a section of mature bamboo with narrow strips of bamboo raised by wooden wedges to create the strings. These instruments are known as the *kolesing* in Ilongot or *patting* in Ifugao.

Lutes (*hegalong* in T'boli and *kudyapi* in Bukidnon) are common, but much smaller than European versions and they usually have two strings.

Bow-played instruments include several types of spike fiddles (named because they have a spike coming out of the bottom on the body), including the *duwagey*, used by the Bilaan, and the *biola*, used by the Tausag. Spike fiddles have no fixed fret but fingers act as a moveable fret.

Jew's harp is the common name given to a small lyre-type instrument where the string is held between the teeth and struck with the finger and the tone of the sound is altered by changing the shape of the mouth around the string.

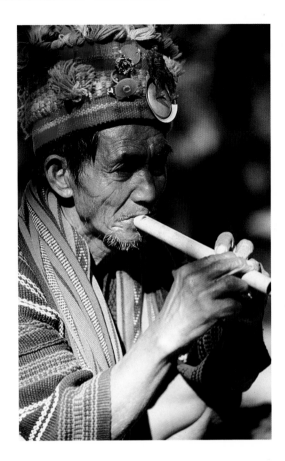

Above: The indigenous orchestra is varied, but all tribes use the simple bamboo flute as an integral instrument. These are easily carried to the rice terraces where tunes can cheer up a long hard day of planting or harvesting.

Percussion

Idiophones (instruments which vibrate to produce a sound when shaken, struck or scraped) or percussion instruments are used a great deal.

The *kagul* of Mindanao is one of the largest indigenous instruments. Five logs up to 2.5m (3 yards) in length are shaped and suspended, then struck with sticks to produce a range of tones. There are two players, one for the bass and another for the melody.

Bamboo tubes with seeds inside act as background percussion, while the bamboo 'buzzer' (*balingbing* or *bunkaka* in Kalinga) is a bamboo tube split at one end. Tapping the split end against the player's palm produces the sound. The buzzer is supposed to be particularly effective in driving bad spirits away, especially when groups of people get together to play it.

Metal gongs (*gangsa* in Igorot, *agung* in Manobo) are the most important idiophones and common to all tribes. In the south they generally have a boss, while in the north they are flat. The *kulintang* is a series of eight

Festivals – January to April

Look just about anywhere in the Philippines at any time of year and there'll be a festival or fiesta. The Christian calendar is crammed with Saints' Days in addition to the major celebrations of Easter, Assumption Day and Christmas. The indigenous mountain people have also judiciously guarded their own cycle of celebration that has been enthusiastically embraced by the rest of the Filipino population in the last couple of decades. In many festivals, religious and secular motifs collide in happy combination. Whatever Filipinos are celebrating they do it with unbridled gusto, so don't expect to remain a spectator for very long!

Ati-Atihan in Kalibo on Panay Island (third week in January)

One of the most colourful and action-packed festivals, Ati-Atihan commemorates a land deal agreed between the local Ati king and Borneo chieftains. The Atis would paint their faces and dance and sing for their foreign guests and this is re-enacted with dancers blackening their skin and donning elaborate costumes, masks or face paint. Bands of musicians march through the streets pounding on drums, setting a rhythm that fuels the whole day. After the arrival of the Spanish, the festival incorporated honour to Santo Niño. Ati-Atihan has spawned many look-alikes around the country.

The Procession of the Black Nazarene in Quiapo, Manila (9 January)

Quiapo comes to a standstill when the effigy of the Black Nazarene is paraded through the streets. Touching the statue of Christ carrying the cross is considered very lucky, so the crowds push and mill around hoping to get close.

Sinulog in Cebu City, also in parts of the Visayas (18–19 January)

The largest celebration of the year, with grand parades on land and water, plus cultural exhibitions. The reverential religious procession honours Santo Niño.

Chinese New Year (January or February)

Once only celebrated by the Chinese community, this festival has become popular throughout the country. The Parians of Manila and Cebu City have the most authentic dragon dances and firecracker displays.

Nuestra Señora de la Candelaria – Iloilo City (2 February)

Our Lady of the Candles sees thousands of people walking in procession through the streets behind the miraculous statue of the Virgin Mary, lighting the night sky with candles.

Paraw Regatta between Iloilo City and Guimaras Island (late February or early March)

This race recreates the historic journey of Malay traders arriving from Borneo in traditional *paraw* craft.

Moriones in Marinduque (April)

The conversion of the Roman Longuinus, the centurion who pierced the side of Jesus as he hung on the cross, is depicted with colourful costumes and masks. The beheading of Longuinus is the climax of the celebrations.

Kaamulan Festival in Cagayan de Oro, Mindanao (late February into March)

The native peoples of Mindanao meet together to strengthen their bonds with traditional dance, music and the telling of epic tales.

Cutud Lenten Rites in San Fernando, Pampanga (Easter)

Certain adherents to the Christian faith re-enact the crucifixion. Penitents practise self-flagellation, whipping with burlap rope to break the skin, and allow themselves to be pinned to the cross through their palms.

The Procession of the Black Nazarene in Quiapo, Manila (Easter)

The effigy of the Black Christ is paraded through the streets on its second trip of the year.

Lenten Festival of Herbal Preparation in San Antonio, Siquijor (held on Black Saturday, the day before Easter)

Herbalists and traditional healers from throughout the Philippines gather together in a ritual of Tang-Alap, to create a powerful concoction that forms the basis of other potions that they will make during the year.

Festivals – May to November

Viva Vigan Festival of the Arts in Vigan (first week in May)

Living history comes to Vigan with performances of traditional *zarzuelas*, exhibitions and folkloric performances amongst other offerings.

Kalabaw Races at Pavia, Panay Island (early May)

Water buffalo are primped and preened before they become the stars of a series of races.

Flores de Mayo/Santa Cruzan – Nationwide (throughout May)

The Virgin Mary becomes the centre of attention in Christian villages, towns and municipalities. Each place has a parade with the young women of the community shedding flowers in the path of the statue of the Virgin as she is carried through the streets. In the evening young ladies are escorted by their beaus, re-enacting the finding of the Holy Cross by St Helena. Beauty pageants are also held to choose the queens of the festivals.

Pahiyas sa Lucban in Lucban, Quezon (15 May)

Throughout Lucban houses are festooned with multicoloured decorations, called *kiping*, made of rice flour and rice paper.

Independence Day (12 June)

It's interesting that Filipinos celebrate Independence Day on the day Aguinaldo declared independence from the Spanish in 1898, not the day they became officially independent from America (which was 4 July).

Parada ng Lechon in Balayan, Batangas (24 June)

A roast pork festival may sound kind of strange, but fancy-dress porkies are paraded around the town before the animals are roasted and everyone sits down to eat. The festival coincides with the feast of John the Baptist, patron saint of the city.

Tacloban Pintados Festival in Tacloban City (29 June)

The Pintados celebrates the old ways of the warriors with their ornate tattoos (earned through head-hunting triumphs) and tribal dances. For most the tattoos aren't real; today body painting emulates what would have been permanent marks.

Sandugo Festival in Tagbilaran City (1–2 July)

This fiesta celebrates the *sandugo* (one-blood) accord between Legazpi and Datu Sikatuna. There's street dancing, a martial arts event and the Miss Bohol Sandugo Beauty Pageant.

Kinabayo Festival in Dapitan City (25 July)

The European Moorish-Spanish wars are commemorated here, particularly the Battle of Covadonga when the Spanish took a stand against the Saracens and a miraculous apparition of St James appeared to rally the Christian troops.

Peñafrancia Viva la Virgen in Naga City (third week in September)

A nine-day extravaganza combining religious themes around the Virgin of Peñafrancia and older cultural traditions, with a sunset river parade bringing the whole thing to a climax.

Zamboanga Hermosa Festival in Zamboanga City (10–12 October)

This regatta with a difference sees the *vintas* (native boats of Zamboanga) in races, alongside a whole host of land-based activities in veneration of Nuestra Señora Virgen de Pilar.

Masskara Festival in Bacolod City (1–21 October)

Masks with smiling faces were first used to cheer people up during hard times. Today, the tradition carries on, along with singing, dancing and beating drums.

Lem-Lunay Festival – Lake Sebu, Mindanao (second week in November)

Mindanao's T'boli peoples get together and enjoy horse fighting.

gongs in a row with a varied tone scale, very similar to instruments from Indonesia to the south. In the north two conical drums form the rhythm section to which flat gongs are added. This formation is more influenced by the drums of China and surrounding countries.

Following page: The Masskara Festival at Bacolod is a chance for everyone to wear a happy face. The masks symbolize the sunny nature of the peoples of Negros Occidental in the Visayas and the festival is a time when people forget their everyday worries and just have fun.

Voice

Vocal renditions are common to all the tribes because of the oral traditions of the indigenous peoples. There's a great deal of improvization within vocalization and song creation because songs reflect the singer and the storyline. Chanting, speech, whistles and trills all punctuate the songs. The *sindil* – a verbal debate that is sung back and forth between two protagonists in front of a live audience – is unique to the Tausug of the Sulu region.

The Spanish Era

Kundiman was a particular style of song that developed in the early 19th century. Ostensibly, the songs tell of broken romance or unrequited love, but *kundiman* was also used as a tool to foster nationalist feelings during the era when Filipinos were increasingly hoping for independence.

The *rondalla* is still a popular musical form used to accompany folk dances and choral performances, and combines Spanish guitars with native lutes. Five instruments of varying sizes make up the ensemble.

Classical Music and Dance

The classics have a small but very vibrant heartbeat in the Philippines, helped in the 1960s and 70s by Imelda Marcos's interest in the arts. She was instrumental in making monies available for the Philippine Cultural Center. All the major arts companies perform here. Filipinos contributing to the western classical music genre include Antonio Molina (1894–1980) and Felipe Padilla de Leon (1912–92), while José Maceda (1917–2004) is credited with breaking with tradition and working on avant-garde Filipino classical pieces.

Classical dance training arrived in the Philippines as late as the 1930s. Choreographers Leonor Orosa-Goquingco (whose *Filipinescas: Life, Legend and Lore in Dance* was performed around the world in the 1960s), Remedios de Oteyza, who is known for her abstract ballet, and Rosalia Merino-Santos, mother of modern dance, have shaped the genre. Leading performers include Maribel Aboitiz, Eddie Elejar, and Lisa Macuja.

The national folk dance of the Philippines is the *tinikling*, where a couple of dancers hop between bamboo poles that are banged together in rhythm, rather like a form of musical hopscotch.

Modern Filipino Music

During American rule, the Philippines enjoyed unadulterated access to American popular music, from traditional jazz to swing. After independence this trend continued into the rock and roll and pop eras. However, on the back of this universal trend, a home-grown popular genre is thriving. Original Pinoy Music (OPM) refers to pop tunes originating in the Philippines and it has spawned a string of artists, plus more recent genres such as Pinoy rap.

Karaoke/Videoke

While the rest of the world may not consider karaoke or videoke art forms, one can't ignore the profound importance of this pastime in the Philippines. In the run-up to the elections in May 2007, TV channels filmed rival candidates in singing competitions – forget about debating policy! Filipinos love to sing and even more so with a microphone in hand, and nobody cares whether the rendition is in tune or not.

Arts and Crafts
Crafts

The indigenous peoples of the Philippines are excellent craftspeople. Everyday items are raised to an art form, with their traditional colours and patterns reflecting their exact tribal background.

All these crafts are still very much alive and well, with north Luzon and Mindanao being particularly important regions.

Right: Weaving is a long-established traditional craft. Original fibres included abaca (hemp), pineapple fibre or grasses as at this small workshop, but today the majority of items are woven out of cotton.

Weaving and textiles are the work of a family's wealth was counted in textiles and these were given as dowry gifts at weddings and as offerings to the gods. Hand-spun and dyed with colours produced from the land around them, the *ikat* cloth is produced on a back strap loom, which allows a finished length of up to 3.5m (4 yards), with a maximum width of around 75cm (30in). For wider items such as blankets, separate lengths of fabric are simply sewn together. Patterns are based on a line created in the warp, and there are innu-

merable regional variations, including those between the Kalinga, Ibaloi and Ifugao tribes who live in adjoining regions of the north. Cotton was not introduced into the highland regions until the late 19th century, so before then natural fibres and barks were woven; this is still the case with abaca (hemp) or banana leaf fabric.

Ikat fabrics were reserved for funerary rituals amongst the Ifugao (where the body is wrapped in many metres of material) and Isinai tribes. In a different ritual, the Tinguan hang hand-woven fabric above the body.

The T'boli make a cloth called *t'nalak* through a complicated tie-dye process – traditional motifs are frogs (fertility) and dancing men (rain). Vivid colours and intricate patterns are a feature of Sulu weaving, while the Bagabo use glass beads as decoration on their woven fabrics.

Pineapple cloth was a prized fabric in late 19th- and 20th-century Spanish towns. This was finished with exquisite embroidery by the Chinese. Items like this are now rare and expensive.

Basket-making is the other main craft. In tribal regions basket-making is a man's task and natural fibres like rattan are fashioned into mats for sleeping on or for drying rice, or the *pasiking*, a form of woven backpack. All the tribal peoples wear woven hats to protect against the strong sun – the salakot hats (traditional straw hats worn by farmers) of the Bontoc region are particularly fine. The texture of the weaving ranges from hard for protective items to soft and supple.

Working in Wood

It's a little-known fact that many Filipino craftspeople now serve as ice-sculptors on cruise ships, so skilled are they at carving. Wood is fashioned into everything from kitsch water buffalo to magnificent household furniture. In the Cordilleras, wooden *bulul* are protectors of the

harvest. These are often seated figures or figures with arms outstretched and they are usually found in pairs.

With the coming of Christianity, carved *santos*, or figures of the saints, became important artistic works. Initially they were imported but soon local skilled Filipinos began to carve their own. The finest had ivory hands, feet and faces. Ecclesiastical paraphernalia, from pews to confession boxes to ornate altars, decorated the magnificent churches and wealthy colonial families also commissioned items such as a *santo* for their own private altars.

Pottery

The Manunggul Jar (c900BC) discovered in Palawan indicated a long history of fine work in clay, though recently ceramics have become more functional than fine, the terracotta Pagburnayan pottery from Vigan being a case in point.

Arts

The indigenous people of the Philippines have a strong oral tradition, having never developed a medium that would store the written word for very long. History was written on leaves and bark that rotted after a few years. The Spanish burned many of these fragile manuscripts when they took control of the area.

Writing

The first Spanish secular texts were the *corridor* – ballads of chivalry that were popularized in the homeland and spread across the Spanish colonies. Francisco Baltazar was the first major Filipino poet writing in Tagalog. His *Florante at Laura*, published in 1838, is a disguised criticism of Spanish rule. Pedro Paterno wrote the first novel in Tagalog, *Ninay*, in 1907.

Left: Pottery and weaving are two crafts of northern Luzon; the rich colours have traditionally been produced from naturally occurring dyes and the patterns are specific to a group or region.

Jose Rizal wrote *Noli Me Tangare* (Touch Me Not) (1887), and sequel *El Filibusterismo* (1891), about the evils of the colonial system in his home country while travelling through Europe. The books were not published in the Philippines at the time, but the texts have long been seen as the seeds of revolt against Spanish rule. His last poem, *Mi Último Adiós*, was written just before his execution. Twentieth-century writers in English include N V M Gonzalez, Jose Garcia Villa and Edith L Tiempo.

Mainstream Art

Throughout the early Spanish era, art took its inspiration from religion with ornate altarpieces or scenes from the Bible or the lives of the saints. It was only in the 18th century that secular themes began to become popular.

Damian Domingo was not a trained artist but he broke the mould. His work marked a major departure from religious themes. Some of his hand-painted illustrations, part of a collection called *Album de trajes*, are on display at the Ayala Museum in Manila. Domingo founded the Art Academy of Manila in 1821 – he was the first artistic director, and, for a while, the only member.

In 1884, Filipino art broke into the international mainstream when Juan Luna won the gold medal at the National Exposition of Fine Arts in Madrid, and compatriot Félix Resurrección Hidalgo the silver medal. In the early 20th century Fernando Amorsolo, Fabian de la Rosa and Jorge Pineda concentrated on romantic landscapes, and in the 1920s Victorio Edades introduced modernism to the Philippines. This has produced a healthy crop of modern artists, from Lee Aguinaldo and Fernando Zobel in the 1960s and 70s to Bernardo Cabrera (BenCab) and Manny Garibay today.

The leading sculptor of the American era was Guillermo Tolentino, whilst Napoleon Abueva brought modernism in the 1950s. Eduardo Castrillo heads modern names with his monumental metal sculptures (including the Heritage of Cebu Monument in Cebu City). Others include Solomon Saprid and Abdulmari Imao who interprets Islamic traditional designs for the modern era.

Theatre

The Spanish art form *zarzuela*, a play with music, saw a metamorphosis into Filipino *sarswela*, which became the first native theatrical genre. They were used as entertainment for the masses with their saucy storylines, but were also an outlet for frustration against the yoke of colonialism. Some authors were tried by the Americans for inciting nationalism. Passion plays, or *senakulo*, are also performed in venues all across the country.

Mummies

Amongst the many ethno-linguistic groups in the Philippines, the Ibaloi – inhabiting a small area of the Cordillera Mountains around the modern town of Kabayan in Benguet province – were the only ones who practised mummification. The practice was reserved only for their royal family and religious leaders.

Scientists are divided about when the practice became fashionable, and the age of the mummies themselves. Some hypothesize that mummification began from around 200BC, though many put the dates of the discovered mummies at between 1200 and 1500AD. When the Spanish arrived they acknowledged the practice was taking place and chronicled it, but successfully stamped it out. The mummies remained concealed from the outside world until the early years of the 20th century.

It's thought that the subject would participate in the process by drinking salt water in the hours before death to flush fluids from the system. After death the body was set high over a fire to dry out the flesh, almost in a form of smoking, and herbs were rubbed into the flesh to aid the process. Unlike Egyptian mummification, the internal organs of the Ibaloi were left in the body. After many weeks of slow smoking – the process could have taken up to two years – the completed mummy would be placed in a hand-carved wooden coffin and, after an elaborate burial ritual, would be put to rest in a remote cave. Most of these caves were

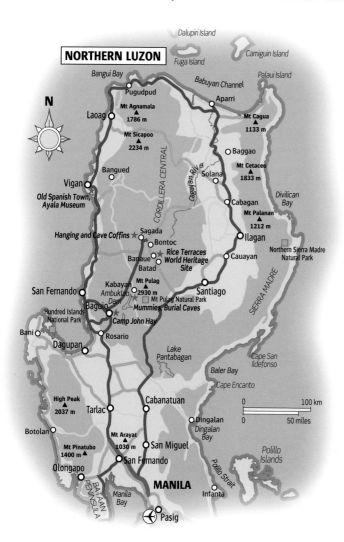

NORTHERN LUZON

Dalupiri Island
Fuga Island
Camiguin Island
Palaui Island
Bangui Bay
Babuyan Channel
Pugudpud
Aparri
Mt Agnamala
1786 m
Laoag
Mt Cagua
1133 m
Mt Sicapoo
2234 m
Baggao
Bangued
Solana
Mt Cetaceo
1833 m
Vigan
Cabagan
Divilican Bay
Old Spanish Town, Ayala Museum
Mt Palanan
1212 m
CORDILLERA CENTRAL
Cagayan River
Hanging and Cave Coffins
Sagada
Ilagan
Bontoc
Northern Sierra Madre Natural Park
Banaue
Rice Terraces World Heritage Site
Cauayan
Batad
Kabayan
Mt Pulag
2930 m
San Fernando
Ambuklao Dam
Mt Pulag Natural Park
Santiago
Baguio
Mummies, Burial Caves
SIERRA MADRE
Hundred Islands National Park
Camp John Hay
Bani
Rosario
Dagupan
Lake Pantabagan
Cape San Ildefonso
Baler Bay
Cape Encanto
High Peak
2037 m
Tarlac
Cabanatuan
0   100 km
Botolan
Dingalan
Dingalan Bay
0   50 miles
Mt Arayat
1030 m
San Miguel
Mt Pinatubo
1400 m
San Fernando
Polillo Islands
Olongapo
MANILA
Polillo Strait
BATAAN PENINSULA
Manila Bay
Infanta
Pasig

N

man-made, making the most of hidden and inaccessible spots, though some natural caverns were considered suitable. All are up at around 2200m (7218ft)
in altitude.

To date, 200 man-made burial sites have been discovered, of which 15 contained mummies; a total of 28 individuals. Scientists hope that there may be more than
100 in total. Many mummies were not actually found in
caves but were used in circuses and side shows, including that of Apo Annu, a tribal leader whose flesh still
bears the distinct and ornate tattoos of a head-hunter
warrior (see page 81 and Head-hunting section below).

The mummy caves and their contents have now been
designated as national treasures by the Philippine government, but these fragile bodies are still not secure.
UNESCO have added them to the organization's endangered list because of the continued threat of looting and
changes in environmental factors likely to result in the
decay of the mummies.

How To Get To The Sites

A few known sites, where you can see mummies in situ,
are open to the public.

Timbac Caves have the best-preserved mummies in
two clusters, but they are over two hours from Kabayan
by vehicle. Bangao Caves are only 40 minutes on foot,
but the mummies are not as numerous or well preserved.
Tinongchol Rock has a small collection of coffins and is
less than 30 minutes from town. It's recommended to
engage the services of a guide, whichever set of mummies you decide to visit.

There is a small museum in Kabayan town where two
mummies are on display, along with many cultural artefacts of the Ibaloi.

Animism, Mysticism
and Head-hunting

The tribal peoples of the Philippines were never con-
quered by the Spanish in the north or by the Islamic
forces of the southern islands. Thus their traditional
ways of life have remained little changed for centuries.

They now act as a reliquary for a fast-disappearing animist belief system and they have attracted much attention from professional anthropologists.

Although around 90% of Filipinos are deeply Christian
and only a couple of percent would now choose to class
themselves as animist, this Christianity is deeply
imbued with superstition and beliefs in spirits and spells
that make the Philippines a fascinating place to visit for
anyone interested in the mystical and esoteric.

Animism

Animism is one of the oldest faith systems in the world.
It centres on a belief that a soul or spirit inhabits all
things on the planet, even inanimate objects, i.e. that
the spirit is a universal entity. Spirits, good and bad,
roam the earth and these need to be accorded the appropriate respect. The most common manifestation of animism is the bulul (rice god) of the Cordillera, invoked to
protect the all-precious crop. Carved gods sit amongst
the terraces to ward off bad weather or pests, while a
straw god was always built into the fabric of the rice
store to keep away thieves, mould and rodents. Shaman,
priests and elders have important roles in controlling
spirits and pushing their power in an appropriate direction. Complicated rituals involving chanting, dance and
sacrifices keep the spirits happy.

Head-hunting

Head-hunting is the practice of removing and preserving
human heads and it was a ritual of certain groups in the
Philippines until the mid-20th century. In certain cul-
tures the head is believed to hold the soul of the individual and to capture the head is to capture the essence of
that individual. Head-hunting was a normal practice during tribal wars between the Ifugao, Bontoc, Kalinga and
Igorot tribes. It has also been associated with human
sacrifice in certain agrarian societies, including those in
the Philippines, in order to ensure a fruitful harvest and
promote fertility in their womenfolk. The Spanish could
never stop the practice, but the Americans did work hard
to reduce its incidence.

Left: The rice gods are the most important manifestation of the animist beliefs of the indigenous Igorot peoples of the Cordillera Mountains in northern Luzon. Carved effigies (bulul), complete with their tribal dress, were placed in the fields to protect the growing crops.

Once severed from the body, the head had to go through a complicated ritual process before its power could be invoked. Amongst other things an animal sacrifice had to be made, the head had to be danced around by the menfolk of the village and then it had to be washed in the river. If this was a first kill for the warrior, the lower jaw was removed to become the handle of his *gangsa* (gong) and the head would then be buried in the ground for several years.

In Bontoc society, no man could marry until he had taken a head, and in most tribal groups those who had taken heads were allowed to wear ornate tattoos advertising their elevated status.

The Ilongot tribe in Northern Luzon developed a custom of taking a head after the death of a loved one, to assuage the rage of grief. Anthropologists Michelle and Renato Rosaldo spent many months with the tribe in the late 1960s, just as the practice was dying out. Renato couldn't understand that this usually peaceable and hospitable people could partake in such violence against innocents until the sudden and untimely death of his wife, when the rage that overcame him allowed him some insight into Ilongot logic.

Psychic Surgery

The Philippines has become a centre for psychic surgery, where practitioners open up the body and remove 'disease' or 'bad matter' without anaesthetic. The healer moves himself into a different plane of consciousness to hone his or her powers on the problem area before seemingly removing pieces of flesh from within the body. Surprisingly, the practice is deeply rooted in Christianity rather than in animism. Most practitioners are Catholic.

The phenomenon is a late starter in Filipino history, arriving in the 1940s with Eleuterio Terte, but the most famous psychic surgeon was his protégé, Tony Agpaoa, who earned a huge following during the 1950s and 60s. Though sceptics dismiss the surgery as a simple sleight-of-hand trick, others suggest the power of the ritual alone may be strong enough to invoke a recovery from the patient. One must also take account of the fact that for many poor Filipinos who can't afford mainstream treatments, this may be their only option. Hundreds of psychic surgeons are said to operate in the Philippines today.

Faith Healing and the Witch Doctors of Siquijor

Faith healing also remains hugely popular, partly due to it being traditional to the tribal peoples of the country, but also because it's a relatively cheap option compared to mainstream treatment. That doesn't mean its use is confined to the poor. Imelda Marcos often consulted faith healers during her time in power and it's said that her large collection of shoes and clothing was partly due to the fact that she didn't throw anything away for fear of someone casting spells on her through her discarded belongings.

Faith healers, or *mananambals*, don't perform 'surgery' but use a variety of methods to diagnose and often prescribe herbal medicine to cure a physical condition, or amulets to ward away evil spirits. Traditional faith-healing skills are passed on from father to son. Other practitioners have their gifts 'revealed' to them. One such is Juan Magasalay who uses 'bubble therapy' to diagnose and treat patients. A jar of fresh water rests on the patient and Magasalay blows bubbles into it. If illness is present the water turns dark, an indication, he says, that the badness is leaving the body.

Siquijor Island has a particular reputation for healing and, some say, for witchcraft. Sorcerers can cast bad spells as well as good to set illness or bad luck on a person as payback for some slight or other. And though many faith healers swear that they would

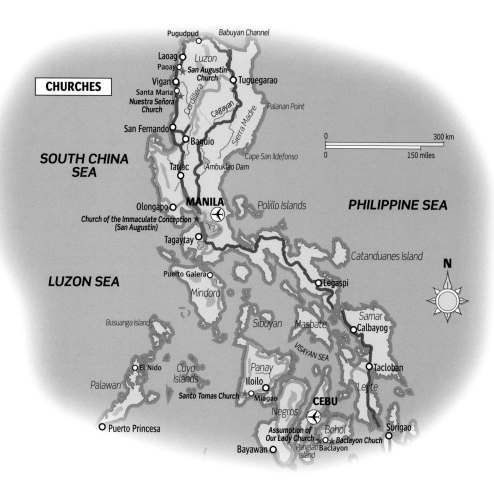

not perform rituals that have a negative impact on people's lives, it's telling that they all have remedies to counteract bad spells. Others say that the spells they create will only work on the guilty (certainly for marital infidelity or theft, where clear moral boundaries are already set by society). They feel that any punishment is God's own will acting through their invocation, and not simply the result of a human desire for revenge.

Churches

When the Catholic Church arrived in the Philippines in the post-Legazpi era, it changed life completely, not only in terms of the evangelical belief system it brought, the education system and the setting up of hospitals, but also in the very fabric of the landscape. The Catholic Church wanted to make a statement about the power of the Holy Spirit and they did – using stone. Nothing like these churches had ever been seen before, where buildings of wood, *nipa* and bamboo had a life-span of around 30 years. The clergy also built high, extending above the tree line, ensuring that Christian imagery was visible from far and wide across the countryside. Most were centres of study set up by one of the Catholic denominations and these church complexes now form a rich historical repository.

Four of the country's Baroque churches now sit in the hallowed list of UNESCO World Heritage Sites; protected for their unique interpretation of European style by local and Chinese craftsmen. However, the Church of the Immaculate Conception (San Augustin) in Intramuros, Nuestra Señora in Santa Maria in Ilocos Norte, San Augustin in Paoay Ilocos Norte and Santo Tomas Miagao, Iloilo Province, are only four of hundreds of excellent period churches.

In Manila, Church of San Augustin and its associated monastery in the heart of the old Spanish city of Intramuros forms one of the most complete complexes in the country. The church was inaugurated in 1604 and was one of the few buildings to survive the destruction of the Battle of Manila in 1945. The remains of Miguel Legazpi are interred here, amongst a riot of Baroque decoration.

Below: Church of San Augustin in Paoay was built by local craftspeople, who added Eastern elements to the European Baroque style favoured by the Spanish colonialists. Four such churches in the country have been recognized by UNESCO for their unique architectural style.

Further north in Luzon, in the province of Ilocos Norte, lie churches that dramatically illustrate the sturdy buttresses typical of the style known as 'earthquake Baroque'. The monumental brick Church of the Assumption in Santa Maria sits on a low hill and was completed in 1769. Long flights of steps flow down on

two flanks. Close by, Paoay Church, the Church of San Augustin, built out of coral stone by the Augustinians, is considered to be the finest of the four and is known as the Borobadur of the Philippines for its crenellated façade with many carved stupas and the decoration on the buttresses. This is also the most pleasing of the sites because the church is surrounded by primped gardens. The church still displays an image of St Veronica, though the Catholic Church no longer recognizes her because it's feared that Veronica was not a person, but that the name came from the Latin *vera icon* (true image), meaning the oldest known images of Christ.

The Augustinians also erected the Miagao church in southern Iloilo province. Completed in 1786, it features a façade with a magnificent carved coconut tree as 'the tree of life' and scenes of daily life of the local Miagaowanons of the time. The church acted as a place of refuge during *Moro* raids.

Other churches, though equally historical, seem less worthy of acclaim, including the beautiful Jesuit complex of the Assumption of Our Lady at Dauis dating from the late 1500s and Baclayon Church, both on Bohol. The church at Laoag in Ilocos Norte has foundations dating from 1612 and was the scene of Marian Congresses in 1932 and 1949.

Left: *The façade of the church of Santo Tomas in Miagao displays the combination of European Baroque and Asian style that is unique to the Philippines.*

Filipino Realpolitik

Putting the spotlight on politics in the Philippines brings several cultural and social norms to the fore – some positive, others negative. The political system is widely believed to be riddled with corruption, but Filipinos are passionate about getting involved.

The oligarchy of powerful families that constitute the Filipino elite is well in evidence at all levels of the legislature, and politics is a family business that can be classed as a kind of benevolent paterfamilias at best and keeping an eye on vested interests at worst. Current president Gloria Macapagal-Arroyo is the daughter of Diosdado Macapagal who was president pre-Marcos between 1961 and 1965. Benigno Aquino Jr., son of Benigno and Corazon Aquino, has just recently been elected to the Senate.

Lower down the political scale, incumbent mayor of Manila, Lito Atienza, wanted to retire so decided not to run in the 2007 elections, but in a bid to ensure that power didn't slip completely from Atienza hands, he backed son Ali for the job. The two were a super smiley double act on the campaign trail but unfortunately Ali was beaten in the only place that matters, the ballot box. Fred Lim, who needed to move from the Senate, but didn't want to leave politics, got the people's vote. Such political musical chairs is the norm here. Candidates slide from mayoral seats to the House of Representatives and back again, once they reach the legal limit for terms served. So the same names do the rounds election after election.

Widows of assassinated candidates often end up in their husbands' jobs, most famously Corazon (Cory) Aquino who led the country out of the dark days of Marcos's rule after Benigno senior's assassination. But even in the 2007 elections, two widows were elected after their husbands died during campaigning.

And despite the international condemnation that was heaped on the Marcos regime after the 'People's Revolution', the Marcos family is still well ensconced in their traditional stomping ground around the family home in Ilocos Norte. Daughter Imee Marcos is a congresswoman and Bong Bong Marcos (Ferdinand Jr.) was governor and is currently a member of the House of Representatives. One look at the Imee Marcos website tells you how important image is in Filipino politics today; she looks like a Hollywood star.

Politicians are a colourful lot. Characters include discredited president Joseph Estrada, who as an actor was known as Erap, the reverse of the Filipino word *pare*, meaning pal or buddy, and Chavit Singson who owns several tigers at his lavish home in Ilocos Norte. The Singson family is one of the most powerful mestizo landowning clans and they've ruled Vigan by Spanish diktat and the ballot box since the 1800s.

Politics continue to be a tough career choice. Over 100 people were killed in campaigning in the run-up to the 2007 poll, schools acting as polling stations were torched and several instances of voter intimidation were recorded (mainly in the southern provinces and often by the Philippine Army). Despite this, Filipinos wear their heart on their sleeves at election time, smothering their homes with election posters and riding through the streets in noisy cavalcades to proclaim support for their favourite candidates.

Travelling in Style

Getting around the country is a major element in the Philippines adventure. Millions of people rely on public transport for all their travel needs, and solutions reflect the natural exuberance of the people.

The Jeepney

Like many things Filipino, the jeepney developed out of practical need. In the initial post-war era there was a need for public transport and coincidentally a surplus of American Jeeps. Enterprising mechanics simply chopped the engine and front cab off the war-horse and fabricated a much more practical rear end that could accommodate 20 or so passengers, and the jeepney was born. But that wasn't the end of the story. The metal panels of the jeepney body were a blank canvas and it didn't take Filipinos long to personalize their wheels;

and boy what a job they've done. Whether it's shiny chrome or a full paint job, the jeepney is never boring, and no two are ever the same.

The huge bulbous nose with its bull bars could be one of the reasons for the rather cavalier national driving style. No one wants to get hit by that amount of metal so jeepney drivers get used to being 'Kings of the Road'. The jeepney is still the backbone of the municipal public transport system and with a new vehicle costing over a quarter of a million pesos and passenger fares around seven to ten pesos per trip, it's easy to see why they keep these 'smokey joes' chugging along as long as possible.

The *Bangka*

The *bangka* is in many respects the jeepney of the seas. A long, slim canoe with bamboo or wooden outriggers and a huge sail, these craft are ideal for inland waters, zipping across the surface. *Bangkas* are used as tour boats, short-distance ferries and cargo vessels and they're a ubiquitous sight in holiday beach scenes.

The English description of the *bangka* is the pumpboat, so named because the small gap between drive shaft and hull allows a constant leak of water that needs to be manually pumped out at regular intervals.

The Tricycle

These small motorcycles with cabs welded to the side are the wheels of the masses in the Philippine countryside, where passenger traffic isn't dense enough to make a jeepney profitable. For just a few pesos one to six people can be transported in relative style, trundling along at around 15kph (9mph), and be dropped off at their doorsteps; though it's no fun in rainy weather, despite the ingenious devices employed

Left: Kings of the road in the Philippines, jeepneys keep the population on the move. The Jeep front with a charabanc rear was invented post World War II, but they've developed a personality that transcends their practical use.

Philippine Airlines

Philippine Airlines, the national airline of the Philippines, is the longest-operating airline in Southeast Asia, having started scheduled services in March 1941, when a small Beech airplane with five passengers made the trip from Manila to Baguio. Today, they fly to 18 cities in the Philippines and 24 international destinations. Their foreign routes include several in the western Pacific, with long-haul destinations including Vancouver, San Francisco and Los Angeles.

by drivers in an effort to keep passengers dry. Hundreds of these cute contraptions crowd around *subungan* (cock-fighting pits) when there's a *sabong*, and they proliferate around markets.

The Language Trail

Over 170 languages have been documented across the 7000 islands of the Philippines and a dozen of these languages have at least one million speakers. Of course, many of these languages are similar within certain geographical regions. However, even given a close association between the syntax of some, diversity over even a small geographical area – such as the region of Bicol for example – is also an important feature. The last census conducted in the Philippines recorded 22 million Tagalog speakers, 20 million Cebuano speakers, nearly eight million Ilocano speakers and almost the same number of Hiligaynon speakers. How does everyone communicate?

How It Happened

Spanish was the official language for centuries – even being enshrined in the Malolos Constitution established after the American takeover in 1899. However, English became the language of education in 1901, thus ensuring it would take on the mantle from Spanish within a generation.

In 1937, the national assembly inaugurated after

the Tydings-McDuffie Act and led by Manuel L Quezon formed a National Language Institute to decide how the language conundrum should be solved. Tagalog was chosen as the country's first native official language – many in Quezon's administration were Tagalog speakers – to the discomfort of Cebuano speakers and others.

The national language had a name change – to Pilipino – in 1961, and experts argue that it is sufficiently different from old Tagalog to be a separate language, having absorbed many words and phrases from Spanish, English and other minority languages.

Today, there are two official languages in the country – Pilipino and English, with English being the language of government, the legal system and of education. A mongrel language, *taglish* (a language taking Tagalog grammar but using English/ American words and phrases), is developing quickly, sucking in words from the modern world.

The Printed Word

The first printing press arrived in 1602, though crude books had been produced since 1593. The first print run was the catechism, or *Doctrina*, that was published in Latin, Chinese and a Tagalog script called *baybayin*. This was a Tagalog Rosetta Stone for philologists and linguists, and proof that Filipinos had a written language before the arrival of Europeans. The extant copy of the *Doctrina* is now in the US Library of Congress in Washington DC.

Left: Tabloid newspapers are produced in all the major Philippine languages, including this one in Tagalog, the second national language of the country.

What´s Your Name?

When the Spanish arrived, only royalty amongst the ethnic tribes had last names — many people were simply known as X, father of Y, for instance; social circles were small and first names sufficed. When *indios* converted to Christianity they very often took a Spanish last name, and suddenly thousands of 'de la Cruz's' and 'Rosario's' began to spring up. As time went on, this proved to be unsatisfactory, so in 1849 the Spanish codified surnames for the whole population. A book of 61,000 suitable surnames was issued and each region given a certain number of names to use starting with 'A' in northern Luzon down through the alphabet the further south you travelled. Thus many Filipinos have Spanish surnames without having a drop of Spanish blood.

Helpful Phrases

Note that Filipino has a formal spoken structure and an informal structure. When you first meet people or you are speaking to a more mature Filipino you should use the second person plural or format form unless invited to use the less formal second person singular. This normally means adding 'po' to the end of the phrase. To people of your own age or younger, the informal should be used. The polite phrases below take the formal form.

English	Filipino	English	Filipino
One	isa	I would like	Gusto ko pong
Two	dalawa	Where will I find...?	Saán po ba may...?
Three	tatlo	Please take me to...	Dalhin po nga ninyo ako sa...
Four	apat	Where can I hire a car?	Saan po maaaring umupa ng
Five	lima		kotse?
Six	anim	How much is it?	Magkano po ito?
Seven	pito	Do you have?	Mayroon po ba kayo ng?
Eight	walo	Can you help me?	Matutulungan po ba ninyo ako?
Nine	siyam	What time is it?	Anong oras na po ba?
Ten	sampu	Yes	Opo (f)
Monday	Lunes	No	Hindi po
Tuesday	Martes	Thank you	Salamat po
Wednesday	Miyerkoles	Good morning	Magandang umaga po
Thursday	Huwebes	Good Evening	Magandang gabi po
Friday	Biyernes	Is this the way to...?	Ito po ba ang daan patungo
Saturday	Sabado		sa...?
Sunday	Linggo	I need help	Kailangan ko po ng tulong
Hello	Kumusta po	Help!	Saklolo!
Goodbye	Paalam	Is there someone who	
What is your name?	Anong pangalan ninyo?	knows how to speak English ?	Mayroon po ba kayong alam
I don't understand	Hindi ko po maiintindihan		na marunong mag-ingles?

Left: Tabloid newspapers are produced in all the major Philippine languages, including this one in Tagalog, the second national language of the country.

What's Your Name?

When the Spanish arrived, only royalty amongst the ethnic tribes had last names – many people were simply known as X, father of Y, for instance; social circles were small and first names sufficed. When *indios* converted to Christianity they very often took a Spanish last name, and suddenly thousands of 'de la Cruz's' and 'Rosario's' began to spring up. As time went on, this proved to be unsatisfactory, so in 1849 the Spanish codified surnames for the whole population. A book of 61,000 suitable surnames was issued and each region given a certain number of names to use starting with 'A' in northern Luzon down through the alphabet the further south you travelled. Thus many Filipinos have Spanish surnames without having a drop of Spanish blood.

Helpful Phrases

Note that Pilipino has a formal spoken structure and an informal structure. When you first meet people, or you are speaking to a more mature Filipino, you should use the second person plural or formal form unless invited to use the less formal second person singular. This normally means adding 'po' to the end of the phrase. To people of your own age or younger, the informal should be used. The polite phrases below take the formal form.

English	Pilipino	English	Pilipino
One	isa	I would like...	Gusto ko hong...
Two	dalawa	Where will I find...?	Saán ho may...?
Three	tatlo	Please take me to...	Dalhin nga niyo ako sa...
Four	apat	Where can I hire a car?	Saan ho maaring umu pang
Five	lima		awto?
Six	anim	How much is it?	Magkana ho ita?
Seven	pito	Do you have?	Kailangan ko ng?
Eight	walo	Can you help me?	Kailangan ko ng tolong?
Nine	siyam	What time is it?	Anong oras na?
Ten	sampu	Yes	Opo (f)
Monday	Lunes	No	Hindi po
Tuesday	Martes	Thank you	Salamat po
Wednesday	Miyerkoles	Good morning	Magandang hapon po
Thursday	Huwebes	Good Evening	Magandang gabi po
Friday	Biyernes	Is this the way to...?	Ito ba ang daan patungo
Saturday	Sabado		sa...?
Sunday	Linggo	I need help	Kailangan ko ng tulong
Hello	Kumasta Ho	Help!	Saklolo!
Goodbye	Paalam	Is there someone who	
What is your name?	Anong pangalan ninyo?	knows how to speak English?	Sinong marunong mag
I don't understand	Hindi ko ho naiintindihán		Ingles?

Island Getaways

Left: *The Shangri-La Mactan has wonderful freeform swimming pools and lush palms only steps from warm seawater shallows and a glorious golden beach; the staple ingredients for every tropical island resort.*

Just as the islands of the Philippines are cast across a vast sea, so its finest hotels are far-flung.

Mass tourism hasn't made many inroads here, so the country excels in quality small island retreats where activities tend to be low-key, making the best of the natural assets, especially under the waves. Boracay is the queen of cool and can't be beaten for those looking for a little action, though even in high season it's hardly packed to the rafters. Elsewhere, your fellow guests may be your only company aside from friendly islanders.

The following selection has, we hope, a little something for everyone. Each has been chosen because, whatever its size or wherever its location, it has something a little special to offer.

Left: The waterfront cottages at El Nido Lagen Island Resort offer some of the most romantic accommodations around, with uninterrupted views out across the islands and islets of Bacuit Bay.

The Peninsula Manila

Peninsula Hotels stand as a byword for quality throughout the world and the Peninsula Manila, affectionately known as The Pen, lives up to the name, sitting pretty on Condé Nast's Gold List as one of the World's Best Places to Stay (2007), and the only Philippine hotel to make it on to the World's Best Hotels 2007 list. This relatively low-rise eleven-storey edifice occupying prize real estate on Ayala Avenue is the *Grande dame* of Makati hotels, having opened in 1976. It sits within walking distance of the chic shopping and dining centre in the Greenbelt and Glorietta Malls.

The cathedral-like entrance hall sums up the whole, oozing a conservative confidence and eschewing decorative 'bling' in favour of acres of luxurious marble in neutral tones offset by verdant 7m high (23ft) Washingtonia palms. The soothing strains of chamber music or soft jazz float through the vast space – the equivalent of four storeys high – provided by the Peninsula String Ensemble or Peninsula Jazz Ensemble discreetly ensconced in the upper mezzanine.

The hotel has 451 rooms and suites designed with 'Filipino elegance' the watchword. The Pen ran a nationwide photographic competition inviting images that epitomized Filipino life in all its many guises. The images of winners Jorem Catilo and Sheila Juan now grace the newly upgraded rooms (a programme started in 2006 and completed in 2008) along with carefully chosen rattan furniture in warm tones. There are elegant marble bathrooms, plus toys like flat-screen TVs.

Service is crisp and professional. This is a well-oiled, top-class team used to dealing with a demanding clientele. The hotel is a social hub of the city for business movers and shakers, for expats, for Manila social glitterati – it's one of Imelda Marcos's favourite haunts when she's staying in the city – and for travellers on the grand tour. There's a real cross section of world population milling around the lobby on any given day. Try a signature Halo Halo Harana dessert whilst you while away a couple of hours – it's a signature of the hotel and over 7000 are served every year!

Below: The grand reception space at the Peninsula Hotel is a meeting spot for the city's movers and shakers; an elegant place for an early evening apéritif or afternoon tea.

Mom's Ultimate Package

The Peninsula prides itself on service and loves to make dreams come true. Just have a look at this 'best of the best' Mother's Day package, proposed at the cost of a mere million and a half pesos (£16,317/€24,256).

- Two nights and three days in the Peninsula Suite
- Transfer to and from home in a Mercedes limo
- Champagne and fruit and cheese platter
- Box of Peninsula chocolates
- Mother's Day flower arrangement
- Vanity basket with La Prairie caviar
- Hair session at the styling salon
- Champagne breakfast delivered to your suite
- Afternoon tea
- Eight-course dinner at Old Manila restaurant
- Private shopping at the hotel's Jul B Dizon jewellers, plus a 500,000 peso shopping voucher
- Chauffeured private shopping at Louis Vuitton with champagne and canapés, plus a 200,000 peso shopping voucher

The Limo Service

Peninsula Hotels prides itself on its fleet of luxury guest cars – started with the Peninsula Hong Kong who have been using Rolls Royces since 1970. The Pen Manila made a marque change, opting for Mercedes-Benz S-Class limousines, though still in the signature dark green livery.

The Manor

A little piece of Aspen or Val d'Isère in the Philippines, The Manor couldn't look less like a tropical island hotel if it tried. With sturdy stone walls, shingle roofs and stacks of pine-wood balconies, you could think yourself in the Alps or in the Rockies, a mountain lodge design stolen from the front of a chocolate box.

It's unsurprising in some ways once you understand that The Manor sits amongst the Cordillera in the north of Luzon. The air is cool by Philippine standards and the surrounding slopes are often enveloped in thick swirling mists, like mountain lodges everywhere.

The interior, too, leans heavily on traditional mountain design – though the decorative elements are taken directly from the art of the native Igorot peoples. Wood panelling lends a warm feel, further accentuated by a huge open fire (only lit in the most inclement weather) that seems incongruous if one checks in under the hotel's efficient air-conditioning system. Studio rooms and one- and two-bedroom suites cater to couples and to families.

The hotel restaurant is an excellent place for a leisurely dinner, in the pretty air-conditioned dining room or large covered terrace. The European chef takes influence from classical cuisine but doesn't ignore Filipino staples, which are slow-cooked to perfection. A cosy bar has live music nightly.

Above: A mountain lodge in the tropics, the style of The Manor offers more than a hint of Aspen or Gstaad in its design. It's a cosy place to stay after a day in the Cordillera.

Around the 695-hectare (1717-acre) wooded compound of what used to be Camp John Hay are a range of activities open to guests (and to the public), the most important of which is the Par 69 18-hole golf course, which has recently been refurbished by Jack Nicklaus. There are stables offering riding lessons or bridle paths for a canter through the woods, mountain biking, a roller-blading rink and a magnificent butterfly sanctuary.

History in the Making

Camp John Hay was originally John Hay Air Base, established in 1903 and named after the then American Secretary of State John Milton Hay. After World War I it became a summer residence for the American Governor General. Though the base was used as a communications station (it broadcast Voice of America across the country) it was mainly used as an R&R centre for American servicemen and their families.

The American Residence, a classical mansion, was completed in 1940, only a few months before the Japanese invaded. General Yamashita used the mansion as a headquarters during World War II, and the base became an internment camp. Those held were mostly civilians, missionaries and miners from the Cordillera.

The Japanese surrender in the Philippines was signed in the American Residence in September 1945 and after the war the base continued to be used by American Forces stationed at sites in the lowlands at Clark and Subic Bay. Camp John Hay was handed over to the Philippine government in 1991, though the American Residence site is still classed as American territory and is used as a summer residence by the US Ambassador.

The hotel has recently created an eco-trail with information about the flora and fauna, and it has also developed outdoor galleries and performance venues.

Shangri-La Mactan

The 'Shang Mactan', as the hotel is known, is probably the finest all-round resort hotel in the Philippines. It has won a raft of awards in the last few years, including 'Top 15 Resorts in Asia' by *Condé Nast Traveler Magazine* (Reader's Choice) in 2005 and 'Top 3 Resorts in Asia' by *Time Magazine* (Reader's Choice) in 2006. Once you're here it's easy to see why. Occupying a verdant 14 hectares (35 acres) on the northeastern tip of Mactan Island with a private 350m (383-yard) white-sand beach, it really is an oasis, with a range of quality eateries and activities, plus a magnificent spa (*see* page 157).

This is a large resort, with 547 rooms, but it never feels crowded. Guests find themselves at one of three free-form pools set amongst clipped lawns or at the 9-hole golf course. You can dive the house reef just offshore or take a *bangka* trip from the jetty to Olango Island with its sea-bird populations, or islands further afield. It's only a 30-minute journey across the bridge to the attractions of Cebu City, known as the 'Milan of the Philippines' for its famed design expertise.

Rooms are spread across two wings. The Main Wing and the newly renovated Ocean Wing offer six different standards of rooms of varying sizes, from 34m² (366 sq ft) to a presidential suite of 216m² (2324 sq ft). Décor majors in contemporary neutral tones but numerous little Filipino touches, from *capiz* shell bowls to native wood picture frames and rattan chairs, hint at your location. You can be sure that these are manufactured locally by Filipino artisans.

The flavours of the world are available at Tides, where several buffet stations make eating easy. From sushi to

Left: The Shangri-La Mactan nestles in ample grounds with a spa, golf course, private beach and its own offshore coral reef; lots to keep the whole family happy.

New York deli-style desserts, there's something for everyone here at the hotel's largest eatery. The hotel also offers excellent Oriental cuisine at Tea of Spring, and mouthwatering Italian dishes at Aqua, their newest restaurant, while Cowrie Cove (*see* page 144), with its romantic waterfront location, serves fresher-than-fresh seafood.

For the Kids

Children are particularly well catered for at the Shang Mactan. Older kids (and adults) have their own café and E-Zone, where they can immerse themselves in the virtual world of electronic games or enjoy a game of pool. Younger members of the family have specialist staff in a colourful 20-module air-conditioned Adventure Zone where they can climb, crawl and slide to their heart's content, while children under three years have a dedicated area with educational toys and games. They also have their own dedicated children's pool.

Green Credentials

The hotel has a commitment to its surrounding environment and the local populace. A US$1.4-million desalination plant means that it creates all the water it needs. A modern sewage treatment plant processes all waste and provides water for irrigation of the grounds and golf course.

The Shang Mactan has adopted the reef just offshore from its beach and is actively involved in a coral regeneration programme in conjunction with the local Lapu-Lapu city authorities.

Pansukian Resort

This exquisite boutique resort sits on one of the most natural of the many Philippine islands – Siargao off the northern coast of Mindanao. Set in an old coconut plantation fronted by a tranquil lagoon and surrounded by ancient mangroves interspersed with sublime beaches, the Pansukian is an ensemble so stunning that it's been featured in the prestigious magazine *Architectural Digest*.

Blending classical Filipino design with Thai, Malay and Cambodian influences, the cottages and villas sit in timeless union with the mature tropical gardens, includ-

ing many of the plantation's mature old coconuts. Wooden pagodas are set at strategic points around the property for shade, but also acting as a focus for peaceful reading, contemplation or meditation.

All the accommodation, from the Garden Cottages, through the Tropical Villas, to the Superior Tropical Villas, have been built out of locally sourced materials, from the polished floorboards to the thatched roofs. Walls are soothing and pale, with accents of terracotta. Local crafts feature throughout, from the relief details of the carved coffee tables or around bedroom mirrors, to the woven rattan of the umbrella stands, and it is these myriad little touches in the accessories that make the accommodation so delightful.

The Personal Touch

Pansukian is the brainchild of a young French lawyer, Nicolas Rambeau. Taking a sabbatical from his busy schedule, he was travelling around Southeast Asia in the mid-1990s when he discovered this corner of paradise and he happily packed up his briefs in Paris to start a new life on Siargao.

All the buildings are his invention and his natural gift for design shines through in every detail of the property, though he has no formal qualifications. The infectious delight he displays in living his life here is apparent as soon as you meet him and his vivacious partner Gai. Great Dane Napo completes the family.

Copra

Copra is the dried meat of the coconut. When the mature nut is harvested the flesh or kernel is removed from the husk and is left to dry in the sun until it has lost most of its moisture content. Copra cannot contain more than 6% water. This hard coconut is then processed to extract coconut oil – used in industries such as soap manufacturing, skin-care products or sun-tan oils. Once the pressing process is complete, the residue, now called copra meal or copra cake, is used for fodder for cattle and horses.

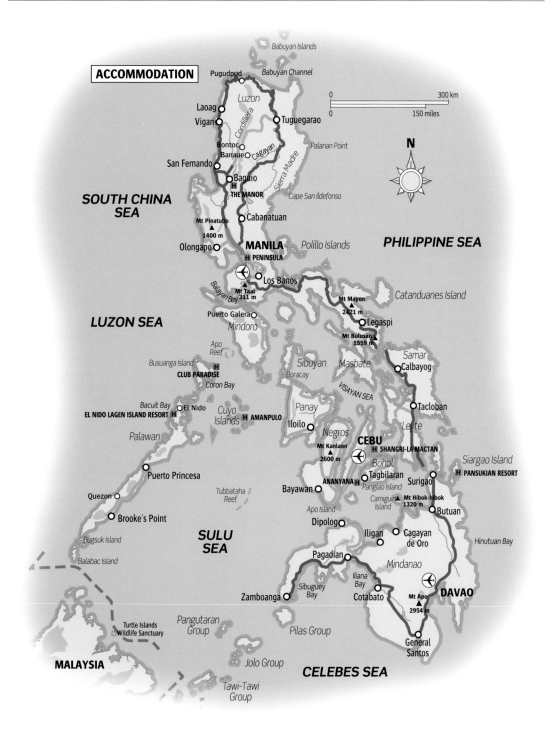

ACCOMMODATION

Babuyan Islands

Pugudpud
Babuyan Channel

Luzon

Laoag
Vigan
Cordillera

Tuguegarao

Palanan Point

Bontoc
Banaue

Cagayan

San Fernando

Sierra Madre

Baguio
H THE MANOR

Cape San Ildefonso

SOUTH CHINA SEA

Cabanatuan

PHILIPPINE SEA

Mt Pinatubo
▲ 1400 m

Olongapo

MANILA
H PENINSULA

Polillo Islands

Los Banos

Mt Taal
▲ 311 m

Balayan Bay

Mt Mayon
▲ 2421 m

Catanduanes Island

LUZON SEA

Puerto Galera

Mindoro

Legaspi

Mt Bulusan
▲ 1559 m

Apo Reef

Busuanga Island
H CLUB PARADISE

Coron Bay

Sibuyan
Boracay

Masbate

Samar

Calbayog

VISAYAN SEA

Bacuit Bay
El Nido
EL NIDO LAGEN ISLAND RESORT H

Cuyo Islands
H AMANPULO

Panay

Iloilo

Tacloban

Leyte

Palawan

Negros

Mt Kanlaon
▲ 2600 m

CEBU
H SHANGRI-LA MACTAN

Siargao Island
H PANSUKIAN RESORT

Puerto Princesa

Tubbataha Reef

ANANYANA H

Bohol
Tagbilaran
Panglao Island

Surigao

Quezon

Bayawan

Apo Island

Camiguin Island
Mt Hibok-hibok
▲ 1320 m

Butuan

Brooke's Point

Dipolog

SULU SEA

Bugsuk Island

Balabac Island

Iligan

Cagayan de Oro

Hinutuan Bay

Pagadian

Mindanao

Zamboanga

Sibuguey Bay

Iliana Bay

Cotabato

Mt Apo
▲ 2954 m

DAVAO

MALAYSIA

Turtle Islands
Wildlife Sanctuary

Pangutaran Group

Pilas Group

General Santos

Jolo Group

CELEBES SEA

Tawi-Tawi Group

N

0   300 km
0   150 miles

Previous page: Sunset at El Nido Lagen Island Resort, and tables are set out around the pool for a wonderful alfresco dinner under the palms, the lights of Palawan fishing villages twinkling in the distance.

Siargao Island

The 30km by 25km (19 by 16 mile) island is one of the most unspoilt corners of the Philippines, with ecosystems ranging from virgin mangrove swamps along the sheltered western and southern shorelines, to tropical lagoons, sandy islets, and ancient stands of rainforest at its heart.

Islanders still live by fishing and farming. The main crop is copra (dried meat of coconut), as it has been for several generations.

Siargao is one of the few islands with a population of wild tarsiers, and they share the forests with the Philippine macaque. The beaches offer nesting grounds for the rare green turtle, while offshore on the east coast are several excellent surfing areas.

El Nido Lagen Island Resort

The setting of El Nido Lagen Island Resort could not be more dramatic. Nestling in a sheltered bay at the foot of a sheer limestone bluff, one approaches from the sea to a scene like James Bond arriving at Scaramanga's secret hideout in *The Man with the Golden Gun* (1974). The hotel is set off El Nido in the heart of Bacuit Bay, surrounded by 45 other islands and islets, and close to some of the finest diving in the Philippines.

Lagen styles itself as a luxury eco-resort and, of its kind, it's one of the best. In fact, it was a *Condé Nast Traveler's* Green List awardee in 2006 and it does this in a variety of ways. The hotel will ask that you take any packaging that you bring away with you after your stay, to dispose of it on the mainland. However, don't expect to find suitable facilities at El Nido town either. Local foodstuffs and products are sourced as much as possible, including the beautiful hand-woven grass bag that's a welcome gift when you arrive.

Lagen Island has several footpaths leading up through the forest and on to small beaches away from the resort. The forest supports over 100 bird species – including the impressive Palawan Hornbill – plus animals, including the monitor lizard, a population of macaques and the smaller Palawan squirrel. Offshore, snorkelling and diving could introduce you to turtles, dolphins and parrotfish. The resort issues all guests with wildlife check lists and asks that any species spotted be noted, so that they can build up a database of Lagen Island diversity.

The hotel doesn't offer an array of motorized water sports that can damage marine life or frighten animals away. There's a set range of activities on *bangka* tour boats, you can take kayaks or small sail boats to explore the surroundings, or head out with a dive instructor/guide.

There are 51 rooms in total and décor is standard throughout, with *narra* wood floors and antique Filipino furniture and full-length sliding glass doors opening out on a spacious veranda. Forest Rooms and Suites sit in two-storey buildings surrounded by tropical vegetation directly beneath the limestone cliff faces. But the most romantic rooms have to be the individual waterfront cottages, built on stilts over the water with Oriental-style *nipa* roofs and uninterrupted views out across Bacuit Bay.

There's a small sheltered beach on hand and a decent-sized pool, but why bother swimming here when there are amazing tropical lagoons just a short boat ride away.

The Landscape of Bacuit Bay

These incredible limestone islands were created as a by-product of tectonic plate movement between the Indian Continent and Mainland China around 60 million years ago, though the original limestone layer was laid down around 190 million years before this. Though geographically part of the Philippines, Palawan sits on a different tectonic plate – the Eurasian Plate on which Mainland China sits. It broke away from the bulk of this plate around 40 million years ago and has been slowly drifting eastwards ever since.

Discovery Shores

The country's most recent high-class hotel opened its doors in March 2007, and it has already caught the attention of the folks at Small Luxury Hotels of the World who have awarded it their seal of approval and promptly added it to their select portfolio. Discovery Shores is the first in the Philippines to gain this accolade.

Discovery Shores sits at the north end of White Beach, Boracay, on a fantastic palm-shaded stretch of sand. When it came to planning, the management at Discovery Hotels engaged famous Filipino designer 'Budji' Layug to make his mark. Layug and his design team deliberately turned their backs on traditional Southeast Asian chi-chi tropical styling and the result is breathtaking; there's nothing remotely similar to this ultra-cool design anywhere else in the country. Like a gleaming oceanliner turned inside out or a 21st-century Greek village, the clean, pale lines of the buildings tumble down over a small rocky outcrop to meet the fine white sand of the beach. A vast, crisp façade is enhanced with frosted glass and burnished metal trim.

The 88 spacious suites continue the pale and sophisticated theme, with a predominance of stone, pale ceramic and tropical woods, in a style that blends the Art Deco with the now. The suites are open-plan with a huge central bed. CD players and huge flat-screen TVs are the toys you need for in-room entertainment.

Small Luxury Hotels of the World

Small Luxury Hotels of the World (SLH) is an umbrella organization of over 400 hotels in more than 65 countries, in locations ranging from major cities to island hideaways. All SLH hotels (www.slh.com) offer an unrivalled quality of stay and a unique experience – from the vineyards of Bordeaux to the plains of Africa.

In 2007, the Brand Status Index survey put SLH at the top of the list for luxury hotel brands based on respondent feedback. Guests felt that the SLH was the brand that most consistently attained its own high standards.

Below: The clean architectural lines of Discovery Shores mark a departure from tropical design and offer a contemporary take on luxury, only feet from the glistening White Beach of Boracay.

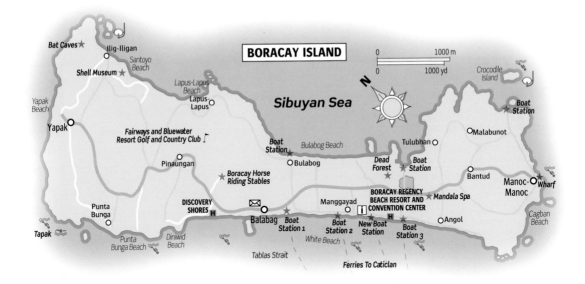

The refreshing sound and movement of water is a signature feature of Discovery Shores. A 14m (46ft) waterfall flows with the natural terrain, descending into a pool that feeds flowing conduits on either side of the main walkway.

The public face of Discovery Shores opens directly onto the beach. Sands Restaurant offers dishes from around the world, while neon-lit Sandbar is the new cool place for cocktails. From the Mandala Spa on the upper floor there are views of the *bangkas* plying the waters just offshore.

The Designer

Antonio 'Budji' Layug was born in 1950 into a furniture-manufacturing family. He studied at the New York School of Interior Design but rediscovered his love of natural materials on his return to the Philippines. His fame as a furniture designer stems from this appreciation of the organic and he has developed into a major force in interior design by combining the natural with the state of the art. He has worked on several major projects worldwide, including Walt Disney World®'s Polynesian Resort in Florida and Little Dix Bay on Virgin Gorda.

Boracay Regency Beach Resort and Convention Center

If you want to stay at the epicentre of the Boracay action, you can't get a much better location than the AAA-rated Boracay Regency Beach Resort and Convention Center. Having the widest frontage of any hotel on White Beach, it's a stunning spot. Restaurants, shops and bars also surround the hotel, so it's only a few sandy steps to whatever your heart desires.

The hotel comprises three phases, but the earliest rooms in the south wing have benefited from refurbishment in late 2007. Older-style rooms are bright with tropical décor. Each of the two early wings has its own courtyard swimming pool. However, the impressive new garden wing was unveiled in mid-2007 and, though furthest away from the beach, it offers the most elegant accommodation. Cool, dark woods and marble and

Right: Having the longest beachfront of any hotel on White Beach, the Boracay Regency also features three bijou swimming pools. It's a great location, in the heart of the action.

stone predominate to offer a contemporary backdrop to locally produced design accents, and all the rooms overlook a courtyard dominated by water, with two exceptional pools, a Jacuzzi and central swim-up bar. Book a stay on the ground floor and you'll be able to swim directly from your terrace. The garden wing is also home to Boracay Regency's spa – located on the top floor for utmost privacy.

The hotel has a selection of bars and restaurants fronting the footpath that runs the length of White Beach. Sit at a table at M02 Wave, Prince Hendrik Café or Café Christina, and Boracay life will pass as you relax. Watch honeymooners show off their matching henna tattoos or barter for pearls with the street vendors.

The impressive carved and painted Oriental-style disc at the top of the flight of steps leading to the upper floors of the hotel from the beach seems to be the signature view and is a favourite place for happy souvenir snappers.

Step across the sandy thoroughfare onto the beach itself, where the hotel has massage tables during the day and a delicious buffet every evening (weather permitting). Turn north or south and it's a 2.5km (1.5-mile) stroll to either end of the beach. Why not book a *bangka* trip or a ride on a jet ski?

Club Paradise

Club Paradise might sound a little like the name of a 1970s discotheque but this small resort ticks so many plus boxes in the 2000s. You know you are in for adven-

ture when you land at Busuanga airfield, a dirt strip in the midst of farmland; this is the Philippines at its most rural. Nestling on the 19-hectare (47-acre) Dimakya Island, a 20-minute boat ride off the northern shore of Busuanga, the limestone island has a natural forested peak and a gorgeous 700m (2297ft) long teardrop beach, plus more than a few animal friends to keep you company.

Guests have the whole island to themselves but resort facilities rest on the southern tip, while the rest has been left as a natural park for the benefit of endemic flora and fauna. The waters around Dimakya attract dugongs during part of the year and have been declared a sanctuary for these gentle marine creatures. The wildlife of Dimakya Island is varied, with monitor lizards and Calamian deer, plus a huge cloud of fruit bats that roost noisily in the canopy behind the reception area throughout the day.

The 52 rooms break down into three types. Sunrise and sunset beachfront cottages have wide wooden decks overlooking the golden sand, while larger apartment-style rooms have an island view. Each location has rooms that vary in size for couples up to families of five. Interior décor is clean and contemporary with touches like Filipino island art and accessories.

You can do as little or as much as you want at Club Paradise. Read a book in the hammock on your deck with just the sound of the lapping waves nearby, have a massage at the spa, laze by the pool, head up the nature trail to spot the island's wildlife, go diving with the qualified dive team or take a tour of neighbouring Busuanga and Coron islands, or the Calauit Island Wildlife Sanctuary. The Calamian Islands, of which these are all part, are highly concentrated but are sparsely populated, with a mainly arable lifestyle.

The Dugong

The dugong is one of only four members of the *Sirenia* family – the planet's only marine mammal herbivores.

Accreditation of Hotels and Resorts

Each hotel or resort in the Philippines is accredited by the government. However, the system is complicated and different from the internationally recognized star system, so it can be confusing. Hotels are rated Economy Class, Standard Class, First Class and Deluxe. To achieve the lowest Economy Class standard, a hotel must have rooms at least 18m² (194 sq ft) in area and provide a private bathroom with 24-hour cold water and hot water at set hours, cold drinking water and room service.

Holiday resorts are classified differently, with Class A, Class AA, and Class AAA, plus a Special Interest category. These ratings seem to be based on how many activities a resort offers. To qualify for the highest AAA rating a resort must offer at least four different sports or recreation facilities.

There are no measurements of ambience and style, which means many boutique properties don't necessarily get the rating they deserve. For more details see: www.tourism.gov.ph/dot/classification.asp

The dugong's closest relative is the manatee, but they differ in one key area. The manatee has a large round paddle tail where the dugong has a tail like a dolphin. The animals reach around 3m (10ft) in length, with a rounded body that is covered in fine hairs. Forelimbs modified as paddles are used for forward propulsion. The dugong graze sea grasses like cows graze fields. They are extremely gentle creatures.

Dugongs fall prey to sharks and killer whales and were hunted by man for their meat and rich body oil. They are now endangered across all their range – much of Australasia and Southeast Asia – with small, scattered populations and a slow rate of reproduction that makes them even more vulnerable to extinction.

It's thought that the gentle facial features of the sirenians gave rise to the legends of mermaids. Sailors who spotted them from a distance and watched them disappear under the water were sure these were half woman, half fish.

Ananyana

Set on Doljo Beach, Panglao Island, Bohol, you couldn't wish for a better location. A quiet corner amidst 3km (2 miles) of fine white, gently shelving sand lapped by azure waters, you'll have the place to yourselves, save a few fishermen who hand-cast their nets in the shallows. Sun-beds are set out on the 200 or so metres (219 yards) of beachfront, only a few steps away from your room.

Opened in 2001, the Ananyana was at the forefront of the arrival of the boutique hotel industry in the Philippines, and it's become a template for a new generation of properties for whom small is beautiful. The hotel aims high 'to create paradise on earth' for its guests and, if you want a retreat with discreet but attentive staff where you can recharge your internal batteries, then you'll certainly find it here. There's no imposition and no timetable and it's the kind of place that, after a couple of days, feels like home. The minute you walk through the gates and look across the shady gardens to the ocean beyond, you can feel an immediate drop in stress levels.

'Stylish comfort, not elitist luxury' is a phrase the hotel itself likes to use, and it's difficult to find words that better describe the Ananyana. The open-sided lounge area has furniture by top Filipino designer Kenneth Cobonpue,

while the rooms have soothing neutral walls accented by local artwork and Cebu-made design accessories. Plus, with only 12 rooms (10 doubles and two family rooms), you'll never feel swamped with people.

The property's *bulul* mascot sits by the pretty pool area that flanks one side of the restaurant, casting a watchful eye over proceedings. The gardens have sunny spots for tanning or shady areas under mature trees where you can laze in a hammock and read a book borrowed from the hotel's own paperback library.

The spa is a little treasure: an oasis within an oasis where you can enjoy a massage, a facial or a manicure. Everything is designed with you in mind, from the initial citrus foot wash to the opportunity to relax on a chaise-longue lulled by the soothing tones of the fountain.

Following page: Follow numerous celebrities to Amanpulo, an exclusive tropical retreat, where you can luxuriate in your private villa and take dinner at the gourmet restaurant by the pool.

Below: A haven of peace and tranquillity on Duljo Beach, Panglao Island, the Ananyana is a cosy boutique hotel that feels like your own private staffed villa: a wonderful place to recharge the mental and physical batteries.

The Ananyana excels in dive provision. The small number of guests means that you'll be ensured personal service, and if you are learning to dive it's difficult to imagine a better choice. No crowded dive centre, but a quiet area with comfy couches where you can relax and watch the training videos or study the course books. Qualifying dives take place on the house reef – Doljo Point – just a couple of minutes offshore by boat where the wealth of sea life is awe-inspiring.

If you are already qualified, the staff here can guide you to some of the country's finest dive sites, including Pamilacan Island, The Black Forest northeast of Balicasag Island, and Puntod Wall, off Puntod Island, with its beautiful coral garden.

Amanpulo

Superlatives are scattered throughout all these hotel reviews, but the truth is that Amanpulo tops the lot – the whitest beaches, the clearest waters and an almost legendary reputation. *Aman* is the Sanskrit word meaning 'peace', while *pulo* is Pilipino for 'island', and this is certainly a haven on earth, if not heaven on earth.

The list of Amanpulo's celebrity guests is impressive but the hotel stays suitably discreet about exactly who has spent time here, protecting the privacy of those more usually in the limelight. The glossy magazines have no such qualms and have named Naomi Campbell, Mariah Carey, Claudia Schiffer, Tom Cruise, Michelle Pfeiffer, Robert de Niro, and Diana Ross as past guests. Luxury is a draw to be sure, but another big plus is that it's practically paparazzi-proof.

Amanpulo is set on one of a tiny island group incorporated into the Cuyo Islands, set between northern Palawan and Panay, almost directly south of Manila. Filipino architect Bobby Mañoso, a specialist in design in bamboo, designed the hotel and it opened in December 1993. Forty individual *casitas* of 65m^2 (699 sq ft) sit in 84 tropical hectares (208 acres). Each *casita* comes with its own golf cart for guests to get around, or you can jump on a bike to explore the island.

The Beach Club and Club House décor have a colonial feel. Here you can borrow a book or a DVD, laze by the expansive pool or enjoy delicious gourmet food at the restaurant.

The *casitas* are spacious and airy with light wood floors and natural rattan, coconut-shell and bamboo furniture, and everything blends to create a relaxing and soothing atmosphere with minimal fuss and clutter. The bathroom occupies over half the area of the *casita* and offers a shower, bath and changing area. Open up the sliding glass doors and you'll find a wraparound deck offering ample sun or ample shade, depending on your whim. What you pay for is the knowledge that no one can invade your space; there's no noise but your own.

Getting to Amanpulo is the start of this fantastic adventure. Check-in formalities are carried out at a private airport lounge before you are flown in a 19-seater plane to the island's private strip around an hour from Manila.

Green Credentials

Aman Resorts play an active role in wildlife protection. The surrounding waters have been designated a marine sanctuary and the beaches are a nesting site for endangered green and hawksbill turtles. Amanpulo staff are working with the World Wide Fund for Nature (WWF) to monitor the laying, remove eggs from the nest and incubate them, tag the hatchlings and then release them safely, to try to improve our very limited knowledge about what happens to these young turtles and where they travel as they mature. Only one thing is certain: that female turtles will return to this very beach to lay their own eggs, continuing the turtle life cycle. Guests are welcome to get involved, including being able to release the babies and wish them luck on their perilous journey.

Right: What more could one ask for? A comfy hammock in your own private tropical garden at Amanpulo, a refreshing cocktail to quench your thirst and views to die for. Heaven on earth!

Shopping and Markets

Left: *There's a wealth of souvenir goodies to browse for on Boracay, including these funky natural beach sandals and straw hats, perfect for the climate and for a holiday state of mind. Many of the woven bags and hats will be made in the Philippines, and prices don't break the bank.*

Shopping for *pasalubong* – gifts and souvenirs – is a real treat, from haggling with a native Igorot for a tribal carving to browsing in a high-class mall for designer luxuries. Whether you intend to spend a handful of pesos or max out your credit cards, there's something for every budget.

The quality of Manila's shopping matches that of any city in the world. From Armani to Salvatore Ferragamo, you can shop at the swankiest stores. But Filipino design shouldn't be ignored – the domestic scene is vibrant, from top-class clothing to art and interior design.

But it's the colourful crafts that most reflect the spirit of this nation. Made with skills passed down through the generations, these hand-fabricated and natural products make a major economic impact for these unique peoples.

Left: Pack light and buy your clothes when you get here – Filipino designers are gaining an international reputation and use fabrics that are perfect for the climate; plus boutiques on the beach are much more exciting than the high street back home.

What to Buy – Best Buys

Filipino handicrafts are found in stores around the world. The nice trinkets you buy to pretty your home are often made by hand around the archipelago, many using natural materials.

Pearls

The Philippines has been the centre of the pearl trade for centuries. Chinese traders had consignments on their inventory at the end of the first millennium and Palawan was specifically mentioned as an excellent source. Today, farms are still located here as well as in the shallow warm seas all around the Visayas, and the country is a major supplier of cultured seawater pearls. Cultured pearls are natural pearls, seeded into two-year-old oysters and grown in controlled environments for around 24–36 months before they are harvested. The Badjao peoples still dive for wild pearls, harvested to provide seed pearls for the pearl farms.

The quality of pearls is measured by a number of considerations, including size, clarity, shape, colour and lustre. Beach vendors on Boracay's White Beach sell pearls amongst other jewellery items, but to ensure quality, visit a reputable retailer.

Shell and Mother-of-Pearl

The inside of the oyster shell is covered in nacre (a translucent material consisting mostly of calcium carbonate). The layman knows it as mother-of-pearl and it's used as a decorative material. The sheen and lustre of this material makes it popular for less expensive jewellery but also for decorative inlay and for small items such as jewellery boxes or small bowls.

Another naturally translucent material, *capiz* shell, is also used for small bowls and boxes.

Art

There's a vibrant art scene in Manila, Cebu and on Boracay, where up-and-coming artists have canvasses for sale at very reasonable prices.

Leader in the field is BenCab (Benedicto Reyes

Pricing Policy

Haggling is the name of the game when shopping in the Philippines. Though fixed prices are found in the shopping malls, elsewhere it's up to you to get the most advantageous price. What the Filipinos find normal practice, visitors may find uncomfortable, but try to remember that bartering isn't meant to be a power struggle; it's a means to reach a mutually suitable price.

Start at around 40% of the first asking price and rise little by little. Interestingly, talking down the very article you have fallen in love with will give you ammunition to keep the price low. Telling the shop owner that you've seen better quality elsewhere is all part of the game. Keep smiling, and if negotiations aren't going your way, you can always walk away. Often you'll find the stall or shop owner will call you back and agree your final price or make a counter offer close to it. Early shoppers may get a better bargain since superstitious vendors like their first transaction to go well as a good portent for the rest of the day.

Don't forget that once you have agreed a price, it's considered very rude to refuse to complete the deal, so don't get into protracted bartering or shake hands with a shopkeeper if you don't intend to buy. Also, do remember as you haggle over the peso equivalent of 30p or 50 cents that many Filipino families exist on very low incomes and paying a few pesos more for an item will be a real help to them.

Cabrera), the current National Artist for Visual Arts for the Philippines, who was born in 1942 and lives in Baguio. BenCab's first international exhibition was in London in 1970 at the behest of actress Glenda Jackson. Others include Emmanuel 'Manny' Garibay (1962–), who has a strong modernist, verging on cubist, style; Cesar Legaspi (1917–1994), who is considered the father of neo-realism in the Philippines; and Claude Tayag, who's also a foodie and has a restaurant in Angeles City. But there are hundreds of other artists out there to enjoy.

Above: This antique store in Vigan combines old wooden santos and intricate carved panels from old Spanish mansions with modern wooden depictions of religious and secular figures. It's worth browsing for collectables in this historic town.

Antiques and *Santos*

The knick-knacks of Spanish and New Spanish (Mexican) families who emigrated to the Philippines between the 17th and 19th centuries now contribute to a small but interesting antiques market. From huge pieces of furniture to small personal items like pretty embroidery samples, sepia-tone photographs and silver cruet sets, there's something for every collector. Antique native art and crafts can still be found but are becoming increasingly rare, hence the high prices. Consult a bona fide dealer to ensure provenance.

Shoes

Imelda Marcos owned thousands of pairs of shoes and ordered many of the same style in a rainbow of colours to match her frocks. She often splurged on shopping sprees in Europe and the States, but was wise enough to shop close to home too. The Manila suburb of Marikina has several factories with outlet stores, including Rusty Lopez and Bobmar, with excellent styling and prices that won't burn a hole in your credit card, with shoes at 50% of Philippine retail prices. Marikina City Hall offers mall tours.

Furniture

Cutting-edge Filipino furniture features in all the up-market design magazines, and the natural materials – rattan, wicker, grasses, etc. – appeal to discerning buyers who want something modern but who are still renewable-resource conscious. Movement 8 is a group of young designers, leading amongst whom are Antonio 'Budji' Layug, Allan Murillo, Ann Pamintuan and Kenneth Cobonpue, who have taken the world by storm since the turn of the millennium. Production centres on Cebu, which has become known as the 'Milan of the Philippines.'

If you are shopping in Manila, visit B at Home, Budji Layug's store where he stocks his own and other avant-garde designs, or About Design. Both stores are in Makati.

Fashion Accessories

Sounds pretty mundane, but one of the country's most important growth export markets is in inexpensive necklaces, bracelets, earrings and/or beaded decorative items to liven up bags, belts or hats. You can buy completed items very cheaply at small factories in Cebu City. Perhaps this is the place to buy the coming season's 'must haves' for all your friends.

The *Barong*

The *barong Tagalog* is a traditional 'costume' of the Filipino male. This thigh-length over-shirt is made of feather-light fibre – maybe silk or *piña* (pineapple leaf) cloth – under which a white shirt is worn. The *barong* works in the same way as many high-tech material shirts, helping to wick sweat away from the skin.

What to Buy – Original Crafts

Tribal crafts in all their forms make the most beautiful souvenirs of your trip to the Philippines. These items are

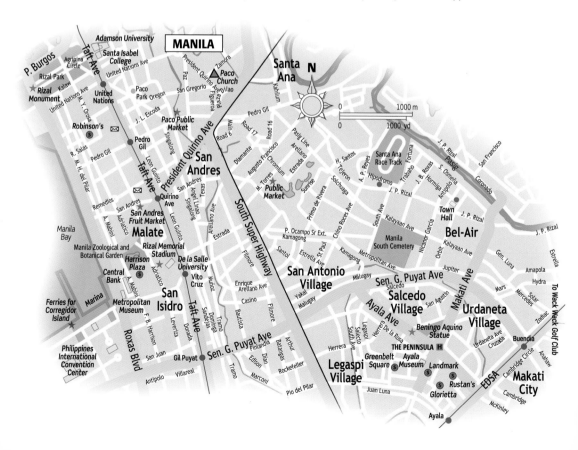

Left: Art flourishes at every level of Philippine society, from established individuals with international reputations to beach or street artists, such as this young artist on Boracay painting scenes on souvenir T-shirts.

Left: Art flourishes at every level of Philippine society, from established individuals with international reputations to beach or street artists, such as this young artist on Boracay painting scenes on souvenir T-shirts.

Harder rattan and bamboo is transformed into trays, room screens, bags and furniture, including excellent patio chairs and tables. Grasses of all kinds are fashioned into decorative items such as ornamental pots and vases to add tropical styling to your interior décor, or take home a hammock for the garden.

Weaving

Weaving and textiles are the other major craft form. Natural fibres such as abaca (hemp) or banana leaf fabric were honed and dyed in natural colours before hand-weaving, and over generations patterns and colours became associated with certain tribes or groups. In the late 19th century cotton was introduced to the region, and the vast majority of textiles are now produced in cotton. However, other natural fibres are making a comeback and have a remarkable texture about them.

Tribal textiles are woven on back strap looms, which limits the width of any given section of cloth. For wider items such as blankets, separate lengths of fabric with repeat pattern are sewn together. Colours incorporate deep reds and dark pink hues plus indigos.

The Cordillera tribes to the north have simple warp and weft patterns with more complicated *ikat* fabrics for funerary rituals. The T'boli make a cloth called *t'nalak*, with traditional motifs of frogs, signifying fertility, and dancing men, signifying rain. In the islands of Mindanao and the Sulu Sea, textile colours are bright and eye-catching and glass beads are often used for decoration.

Working in Wood

Carving is an age-old skill still put to great use. In northern Luzon, small and portable items include simple bowls and trays, sometimes with rattan trim, and miniature *bulul* (rice god effigies), though the genuine article will sit at least 75cm (30in) high and some sit at waist

not merely produced to satisfy the tourist market but form the backbone of practical and useful items used in the home, in the fields and in religious rituals.

Basketware

Natural fibres have been used for generations in the tribal areas to make items used for everyday life, from sleeping mats to bowls and containers. Even the most mundane domestic tool, a wide shallow bowl for winnowing rice, can be ornately patterned and made with great attention to detail. The *pasiking*, a form of woven backpack, makes a great summer fashion accessory for your wardrobe, or buy one of the innumerable styles of hats. Some are so soft that they can be folded and packed in luggage.

height. For transport purposes the density of the wood used will often dictate whether you can include them in your luggage allowance or if you need to have them shipped. Carved masks also depict the spirits. Hardwood furniture such as coffee tables and patio chairs are sold at excellent prices.

In the southern Islamic region, carved wooden boxes – from jewellery box to blanket box in size – are ornately carved or inlaid with brass or mother-of-pearl.

Brassware

In the southern islands, brassware is a long-practised craft form. Influenced by the traditional designs of Islam, and with more than a nod to Arabic styling, ornate carved vases, trays and boxes can be found in antique and gift shops.

Above: Filipino craftspeople transform the most mundane items into things of beauty. Simple carved wooden bowls are embellished with hand-woven grass trim and the result is rustic yet pleasing to the eye.

Musical Instruments

Native culture values music, especially in its many rites and rituals. Instruments are made within the communities who use them and, mainly, from the natural materials in the living landscape. Most of these instruments are light and easy to carry – good for getting back home – though larger items will need to be well packed or shipped.

Carved bamboo flutes are very common – the standard three-hole mouth-played variety, but also more unusual nose flutes. Polyphone pipes or panpipes have several chambers of differing lengths strapped side by side to produce different notes.

Stringed instruments come in a variety of shapes and sizes, with small two-string lutes and spike fiddles being made by many tribes. The Philippine zither has narrow strips of bamboo raised by wooden wedges to create the strings.

You'll have a choice of idiophones or percussion instruments, and these are great presents for children. Bamboo buzzers (a tube of bamboo split at one end, held in one hand and tapped against the other) and hollow bamboo sections with seeds that are shaken to produce sound are inexpensive and fun.

Metal percussion instruments are the most important in the indigenous orchestra. Imbued with a mystical power, they impart a fearlessness and courage in the men about to set out to hunt or fight. The Igorot *gangsa* gong was a symbol of standing in the community. The handle was until recently fashioned from the jawbone of the player's first head-hunting victim and was a valued possession carried with him throughout his life. The *kulintang* is a large instrument, a series of eight large bowl-shaped gongs set in a row. The standard instrument takes two men to carry and play it. However, miniature *kulintang* are manufactured for the tourist market.

Mactan Island off Cebu specializes in handmade modern and classical guitars, plus other lutes and stringed instruments associated with the *rondalla* (*see* page 84). The most expensive versions are manufactured using hardwoods imported from around the world to supplement the native hardwoods like ebony and *narra*. These woods need to be carefully dried for up to six years before they can be used. A top-quality guitar takes six weeks and many man-hours to complete; however, there are less expensive full-scale options or cute little miniatures. If you intend to buy a guitar, get the manufacturer to package it for the aircraft hold – this won't be a problem – because you won't be able to carry it in hand luggage.

Pottery

Several modern ceramicists work at studios in Manila but the day-to-day ceramics tend to be rather plain. The terracotta Pagburnayan pottery from Vigan is a case in point, though the shapes are rather pleasing.

Below: Handmade mandolins, lutes and guitars are a speciality of Mactan Island off Cebu. The salesman will be happy to play a few tunes for you to explain the different styles and qualities of instrument. Musicians will love the opportunity to watch the craftsmen at work.

Where to Buy
Markets

By far the best places to browse for locally produced souvenirs are the general markets, where wares are sold in distinct quarters separating vegetables, meat, fish and general goods, including basketware, wooden furniture and other items, so you can compare quality and prices without having to wander very far. Cebu's Carbon Market and its surrounding maze of alleyways is chock full of Filipino-produced souvenirs and just about every counterfeit product on the international market, including the latest Hollywood releases hot off the copy machine. There's also a tooth puller who visits in the late afternoon who'll wrench out molars for a few pesos. Baguio also has an excellent market, with Igorot basketware and cheaper hand-woven fabric items.

Below: *Markets are the lifeblood of commerce throughout the Philippines, such as here in Baguio, where ladies sell fish caught offshore the previous evening.*

Malls

Malls are big business in the Philippines. All big cities have at least one large covered mall under the SM banner or Robinson's. Manila has several excellent malls, including Greenbelt, Ayala and Glorietta, where international designer names dazzle and wow. Bonifacio High Street at The Fort is the latest up-market shopping district. Tiendesitas is a huge bazaar with over 1000 thatched stalls selling all kinds of goodies for the more budget conscious, and Greenhills or Market Market offers the same kind of fun browsing for food, accessories and gifts.

On Boracay the D'Mall is a more relaxed, open-air collection of lanes and alleyways with shops, bars and eateries that acts as a magnet for evening entertainment. You can shop here for resort-wear and crafts.

Cebu is known for its innovative design in furniture and homeware, and is a centre for the fashion accessory trade, with hundreds of small family-run 'factories.' Mactan Island has a speciality of guitars and other musical instruments associated with the *rondalla*.

Above: *The Philippines has a strong tradition in furniture-making, from rustic tribal items to modern urban chic.*

Almost every mansion along colonial Callé Crisologo in Vigan is a souvenir or antique shop. Antique furniture and collectables from the old patrician family homes make a unique souvenir. Lace, embroidery and old coins make the most portable choices, and there is a range of *santos* to choose from.

For top-quality handicrafts produced by the indigenous tribespeople, the best thing to do would be to visit the area and buy direct; however, there are a few specialist shops that stock a range from several different tribes. The Silahis Center in Intramuros, housed in a period mansion, is probably the best place to shop for textiles, crafts, carvings, folk art and antiques from all corners of the country. Asin Road on the outskirts of Baguio offers several kilometres of wall-to-wall craft workshops selling carved wood items and basketware. You can watch the craftsmen at work while you browse. Narda's in Baguio stocks a good selection of fine Igorot fabrics, furniture and carvings.

Piña Village in Kalibo manufactures *barongs*, gloves, fans and bags in delicate *piña* (pineapple fibre) fabric. You can also buy it at La Herminia Piña Weaving, a factory that makes a range of natural *piña*, and *piña* mixed with abaca, raffia and silk fibres.

Kultura Filipino is a Filipino trade name that sells a range of native-produced handicrafts and clothes in modern styles. They stock a range of perfect tropical and beachwear, furniture and house accessories in natural materials like rattan, hardwoods and grasses. You'll find them in SM Malls across the country.

Jewelmer manufactures jewellery made with high-quality South Sea Island pearls. It has several stores around the country, including Glorietta IV on Ayala Avenue and the Peninsula Hotel, both in Makati, in Metro Manila, and in Cebu City.

Island Cuisine

Left: You can't beat the fresh seafood served in the Philippines, be it the delicious lobster extravaganza served at Cowrie Cove pictured here (see page 144), or fresh fish barbequed over coals at a simple beach bar.

Food is more than simple nutrition for Filipinos; they love to eat, whether it's a sit-down meal with family or friends or a quick snack. Sharing food is one of the great social pleasures for all classes, and not having food for your guests is considered a source of *hiya,* so mountains of it are served at parties and fiestas.

Whether you want a gourmet meal with silver service or a freshly cooked bite at a street stall, you'll find it here. Mom's favourite recipes vie for your attention with the latest creations of international chefs. But whatever you choose you'll find delicious, fresh, home-produced ingredients form the basis of much of Filipino cuisine.

Left: *Fresh chillies* (sili) *are sold in abundance and add a kick to the Filipino hot sauce* sawsawan.

Cuisine

Filipino food is literally a melting pot – one could say a cooking pot – of its many differing cultural antecedents, with dishes and methods from Malaysia and Indonesia mixing with later Spanish, Chinese and American touches. In the major cities and holiday resorts modern influences like Japanese and fusion cuisine offer some of the most exciting options. They are also a popular choice for the Filipino 'in-crowd'. You'll also find a range of foods we could loosely call exotic – from innards to insects – especially in the areas inhabited by the indigenous peoples.

The Basics

Rice underpins every part of the Filipino diet, as well as much of the rural economy, and in many households it's served at every meal, usually steamed or served as aromatic and tasty garlic rice (*sinangag*). Rice is used in sweet puddings and rice flour is the basis to make a range of pastries.

Filipino Specialities

Aside from barbecued (*inihaw*, meaning 'cooking over charcoal') meats, most of the country's meat specialities come in the form of a slow-cooked stew with a zesty or tangy sauce. The dishes are rarely spicy hot, but (*see sawsawan*, page 141) they are full flavoured. Here is a selection of the most popular.

• **Adobo** – meat (chicken, pork, goat or beef) marinated in vinegar and garlic then cooked slowly until the meat is tender
• **Kare-kare** – oxtail stew with peanut sauce
• **Hamonado** – pork with pineapple sauce
• **Kaldereta** – goat in a tomato stew
• **Dinuguan** – stew made with pork blood
• **Afritada** – chicken stew with tomatoes and vegetables
• **Sinigang** – a broth of meat, fish or vegetables in a tamarind sauce
• **Tinola** – chicken stew with potatoes or papaya
• **Arroz caldo** – chicken in a kind of rice porridge broth

The fertile volcanic soil ensures an abundance of crops, with vegetables like carrots, potatoes, taro, cassava and yam, plus fruits including *langka* (jackfruit), rambutan, *kalamansi* – Philippine lime – and the durian, whose sweet taste is offset by its rancid smell. The mango is the most beloved and versatile fruit and even the *Guinness Book of World Records* agrees that the sweetest mangoes are grown in the Philippines. Aside from the mango, the most useful fruit is the coconut. The meat, water and the milk are added to savoury dishes (a process called *ginataan*) and it's also made into sweets.

When the Chinese arrived they brought soy sauce and *patis* or *bagoong* (fish sauce) along with noodles, while the Spanish shipped chilli, tomatoes and corn (maize) from Mexico.

Left: Jackfruits are the largest fruit grown in the Philippines, reaching a massive 90cm in length with a weight of 35kg. The taste has been likened to pineapple but the texture is dryer.

Above: Fish dishes in the Philippines are popular and mouth-wateringly delicious.

No Short Cuts

Filipinos traditionally eat using a spoon and fork, with the spoon acting as the cutting implement if necessary.

Seafood

In all the islands seafood is abundant, fresh and delicious; from massive lobster to plump fish. In restaurants on Boracay or Bohol you'll be able to take your pick from a huge display on ice, and all hotels will have a good choice on à la carte or buffet menus. Even inland, there are mountains of fresh, dried or salted fish in all the markets. *Bangus* (milk fish) is the country's national fish and the choice of the masses, but you'll find ample amounts of *lapu-lapu* (grouper), *galunggong* (mackerel), *hipon* (shrimp), *sugpo* (prawns), *tahong* (mussels) and *pusit* (squid).

Seafood is usually served simply roasted or deep-fried, though it can be cooked in a broth. You can buy it *relleno* (deboned), *tinapa* (smoked) or *daing* (dried) at markets.

Seaweed is also harvested and served as a delicious and nutritious side dish.

Meat

Filipinos are great meat eaters. Chicken and pork are the most popular meats to be found in the Christian regions of the Philippines. Roast whole pig, *lechon*, is a particularly delicious dish, with crisp crunchy skin and melt-in-the-mouth flesh. In Muslim areas goat and chicken are the meats of first choice. Beef is found everywhere.

Meat is an expensive commodity for most households. Even those that raise their own pigs, goats and chickens only slaughter an animal on an irregular basis, so when this occurs no part of the carcass is wasted. In butcher's shops where the meat is always freshly butchered, the less squeamish of you may notice parts of the animal on sale that you wouldn't generally see in supermarkets back home and there are regional specialities that would certainly test the nerve of even the most ardent food lover.

Pinoy Breakfast

Breakfast is a substantial meal, usually a *silog* – this consists of garlic-fried rice and an egg (*itlog*) cooked how you like, but Filipinos like them fried over easy. *Tapsilog* is the above with *tapa* (cured sweetened beef); *tocilog* has *tocino* (dry cured and sweetened pork) as the meat ingredient, while *longgsilog* has *longganisa* (spicy sausage produced in northern Luzon).

Corned beef will often be served in a breakfast buffet, even in high-class hotels. This particular food holds a special place in the hearts of Filipinos. This stems from the period post-World War II when food was scarce and tonnes of this nutritious processed meat were shipped to the islands to tide the population over.

The Humble Egg

Eggs have a particular hold on Filipinos and they have devised many ways to prepare and eat them. Fresh eggs are whisked and added to rice or noodles, or dropped into soups, Chinese style. Hard-boiled *itlog na maalat* (salted eggs), also known as *itlog na pula* (red eggs), dyed a deep pink to differentiate them from normal eggs, are also a popular snack. The eggs are immersed in a super salt concentrate solution for around two weeks before being boiled and dyed, then put out on sale.

One egg dish is infamous in western societies, being so unusual that it has been featured in TV programmes such as *Fear Factor*. A particular delicacy, *balut*, is

boiled duck egg with the embryo developed. Traditionally street food, the embryo is meant to be eaten directly from the shell. It's still a cottage industry and it's never been taken into mass production. Fertilized duck eggs are kept warm and stored to allow the foetus to develop as it would under the mother. After about 17 days, when the claws, beak, bones and feathers are still not fully developed, they are cooked in the same way as unfertilized eggs. *Balut* sellers set out on foot or pushbikes with their wicker baskets, travelling the residential neighbourhoods as they have done for generations.

Snack Time

The Spanish custom of *merienda*, a mid-morning or, more usually, a mid-afternoon snack, is alive and well in the Philippines. In a country where many get up early to travel to work or start work early in the fields, the *merienda* is essential to stop those before-lunch tummy rumbles. City folk might pop to Starbucks for a Danish pastry but other popular choices could be a bowl of *pancit* (stir-fried noodles) or an *empanada* (baked turnovers with savouring fillings, except in Vigan where they are crisp-fried) from a street stall. Home-prepared snacks might include *hopia* (pastries) or *bibingka* (warm rice cakes topped with salted egg and cheese).

The *Sawsawan*

Sawsawan is used to enhance the flavour of any Filipino dish. A form of hot sauce, it is a mixture of *bagoong* (anchovy paste), *kalamansi* (Philippine lime), *patis* (fish sauce), *sili* (chilli), *suka* (vinegar) and soy sauce. Some establishments serve a ready-mixed *sawsawan*, whilst others bring small pots of these ingredients for you to mix to your own to taste.

Left: Salted eggs are a favourite with Filipinos who add them to a variety of dishes from omelettes to noodles (pancit). Salted eggs are dyed a vivid pink to differentiate them from the straight-from-the-chicken variety.

Street Food, Finger Food or *Pulutan*

You'll find charcoal grills on many street corners in the Philippines to satisfy the constant cravings of snack happy locals. The smell of cooking meat wafts temptingly as you pass, but the meat may not be instantly recognizable, and Filipinos have invented some crazy names for some barbecued street foods. Examples include:

- **Adidas** – chicken feet.
- **Helmet** – chicken head.
- **IUD** – chicken intestines.
- **Walkman** – pigs ears.

If all these sound a little too exotic, head to fast-food chains Jollibee (burgers and pastas) and ChowKing (Asian).

Sweets

No meal is complete without dessert, and a sweet-toothed population have invented seemingly hundreds of ways of getting a sugar fix. One of the most popular is *leche flan* (caramel custard), or try *suman* (sticky rice 'lollipops' dipped in sugar or coconut). Two more complicated sweets are *halo-halo* (ice, milk, coconut milk, yam, caramel custard, plantain and jackfruit) and *sapin-sapin* (tri-coloured sweets made up of layers of rice flour, purple yam and coconut cream).

Coconut makes an appearance in other ways. *Buko Pie* (a custard pie/flan with young coconut) is a speciality of the Laguna de Bay area, while *nata de coco* (a jelly-like substance produced by the curdling of coconut water) is popular with Filipinos but another acquired taste.

Drinks

The Batangas area grows coffee, all of which is used locally. Soft drinks include *buko*, coconut water, and a range of fresh fruit juices, though international sodas are available.

The Philippines has its own domestic beer, the quaffable San Miguel, sold in regular, light or 'super dry'. The same company produces a stronger brew called Red Horse.

Exotic foods

The Philippines is renowned for its more unusual foods. Ingredients may be distasteful to some but are delicious to the people who eat them. The indigenous peoples especially make the most of every opportunity to supplement their diets. You'll rarely find these more difficult dishes on restaurant menus. They are more often cooked at home or at local get-togethers, rural farmers' markets, etc.

Dog lovers be aware that in northern Luzon canines are still raised for meat in some tribal regions. *Asocena* is dog meat stew.

In the dish called *pinikpikan* the main ingredient, chicken, is beaten before it is killed to encourage blood to gorge the wings. Beef or goat intestines are stewed to make *papaitan* and the dish is flavoured with bile.

Monitor lizard and frog are two more interesting meat choices, while insects, including beetles, ants and locusts, are popular snacks.

All the tribal peoples have their own firewater – *sebang* (rice wine), *tapay* (fermented rice wine) or *lambanog* (coconut wine). These can be very strong and are said to leave a killer hangover for the uninitiated.

All the international spirit brands are available but Gilbey's gin is pretty good and is home produced, as is Tanduay rum. Tanduay won its first gold medal for excellence at the Exposicion de Gane Bale in Paris in 1876.

Where to Buy Food

Markets are the best place to buy food, and the perfect place to choose tasty items for a picnic. Seasonal fruit and vegetables are piled up in abundance and smoked or dried fish (which is also sold deboned) is ready to eat. Eggs are sold hard-boiled and salted (so you can eat them direct from the shell).

Aside from the cooked snack foods mentioned in the 'What to Eat' section, markets are a source of all kinds of cold snacks to keep in your bag as you travel. Pork rinds are very popular with locals. Groundnuts or peanuts are sold unflavoured, salted, sugared and spiced. Dried fruits such as mango, coconut or pineapple make healthy hunger blockers, along with sunflower seeds and pine nuts. You can also stock up on peanut brittle.

If you are shopping for main meals you'll find excellent fresh meats on sale – every part of the said animal – and a good range of fresh fish.

Most Philippine markets sell live produce too – chickens for eating and layers for eggs, plus, less often, goats and pigs. For larger animals there are regular farmers' markets selling everything from cattle to water buffalo, that ubiquitous beast of burden.

As you travel along the main routes you'll notice stalls selling a range of fresh produce from the fields. Normally this will be whatever is in season or specialist to the region – so for instance in Tagaytay all the stalls sell pineapple – which means product range is limited. Some stallholders sell preserved fruits and vegetables in jars, though it's difficult to know if this has been prepared in a hygienic way.

All the major cities have western-style supermarkets, usually attached to the largest shopping mall. Rustans is a major name. These stock a range of pre-packaged fresh and processed foods, including international brands.

Restaurants

The following selection features a range of the best eateries around the Philippines. We've included a variety of hotel restaurants and private enterprises chosen for the quality of their cuisine, their ambience, and their setting. All hotel restaurants are open to non-guests but it would be wise to make a reservation.

Right: Make your choice from this stall at Alona Beach, Panglao, where the freshest seafood sits on ice ready for your perusal and a discerning eye. Delicious whole fish, juicy tuna steak or muscular tiger shrimp – it may take a while to make your decision.

Cebu
Abaca

American Jason Hyatt spent many years honing his 'chef-ing' skills in Hong Kong before deciding to change his life and open a chic hotel/restaurant here in the Philippines. The result is an exciting new option on Mactan Island. The Abaca menu blends the latest trends in flavours of California and the Mediterranean, while the dining area is a triumph of ultra-swish cool and uncluttered design. You can watch Jason and his team doing their thing in the open kitchen and enjoy a range of wine by the glass while you peruse the menu. Service is excellent but never over eager.

Cowrie Cove

This alfresco restaurant offers waterside tables and a glass-sided air-conditioned dining room. The freshest seafood is served here – so fresh that you can choose your fish, crab or lobster directly from one of several seawater tanks at the kitchens – and it's cooked exactly to your requirements. Cowrie Cove's wine cave is one of the best in the country, with the bottles stacked in a glass-fronted wine vault so you can choose your vintage with confidence, knowing that it's been perfectly stored. The décor is contemporary-meets-island style and the layout offers romantic corners for couples or family tables.

Manila
Abé

Restaurateur Larry Cruz is taking Filipino food up-market at this smart yet welcoming restaurant at Fort Bonifacio, Serendra (the new 'it' place in Manila). Cruz has filled the restaurant with art by his father Emilio Aguilar Cruz (Abé) who was a major romantic landscape artist, newspaper editor and diplomat. Abe's old friends have offered their favourite traditional recipes to the restaurant, but you can choose classic world cuisine such as French cassoulet. The *adobo* is delicious. Serendra Circle is a hub of shops, cafés and restaurants for the Manila well-to-do. Sit at an outside table and you can watch the evening *paseo*.

Right: Café life is thriving on the streets of Manila where you can pick up anything from a genuine shot of Spanish café solo to a creamy mug of Seattle's finest. Filipinos love to snack, so you'll be able to eat at just about any time of day.

Apartment 1B

Maravic Diaz-Lim offers a number of familiar (to Filipinos) favourites with a new twist at this smart address in Makati. Ingredients are cooked to order so the tastes are the freshest, and the food is served in a dining room that Lim hopes is as comfortable and relaxing as any contemporary living room. 'Gourmet comfort food' is the watchword on the menu but lighter appetizing dishes include crab cakes with crispy salads and sandwiches. The breakfast menu is served from 07:00 into the afternoon.

M Café

Contemporary restaurant/bar in the heart of Makati shopping, M Café is the coolest place to sit with a glass of wine, a cocktail, a snack or a full-scale meal. Glass walls and a pale contemporary interior give the inside dining space great light and great visibility, plus of course the all-important air-conditioning, but the covered outdoor tables have a great ambience. The menu has influences from around the Pacific, including crispy spring rolls and a spicy pumpkin curry.

Baguio
Le Chef at the Manor

The best in the Filipino repertoire can be found on the menu here, along with a range of Asian and continental dishes. The food is richly flavoured and served in generous portions. Diners have the option of a large air-conditioned dining room or a covered but open dining area with views across the gardens to the Cordillera foothills beyond. On Baguio's coolest evenings a roaring fire adds a cosy feel and the live jazz from the neighbouring bar adds to the ambience. Light meals and snacks are served throughout the day along with main meals of breakfast, lunch and dinner.

Café by the Ruins

This fashionable haunt is a long-standing Baguio favourite for locals and visitors. Daily specials vary according to the flavours of the market and the menu changes seasonally, but always includes an excellent range of Filipino dishes, including delicious *bangus* and *longganisa*. The muffins and coffee are just as popular pre- or post-town tour or shopping trip. The café building is the former mansion of the Governor of Benguet province and takes its design from the surrounding Cordillera region with *narra* wood and thatch, sturdy locally made furniture and tribal decoration.

Boracay
Bamboo Lounge

One of the coolest places on White Beach, Bamboo Lounge spreads out comfy bean bags and cushions on the sand (tides permitting) and you can eat and drink between sunning and water sports, while watching the sunset, or under the stars after dark. Chill out with the music while you enjoy a range of Oriental-influenced dishes such as steamed *lapu-lapu* with cilantro, garlic, ginger, asparagus drizzled with soya oil, or try an Oriental salad of greens with apple, orange and crispy noodles in a light citrus dressing. A wide range of teas is on offer, or for something stronger try a cocktail or a shot.

Dos Mestizos

Taking the best of the 'Old World' cuisine brought by the Spanish, Dos Mestizos is a diner's delight as many of the dishes have long disappeared from restaurant menus in the rest of the country. Only the most authentic ingredients are allowed in the kitchen, including aromatic olive oils for all dishes. Almost 30 different styles of *tapas* means you can drop in for a snack or order enough for a full meal, but the house speciality is *paella* – they sell it by the weight enough for three, eight or 12 people – and it comes in several different styles.

Pagsanjan
83 Gallery Café

This quirky eatery/gallery is owned by Ernest Santiago, erstwhile doyen of *haute couture* in Manila, who has turned his hand to furniture design and the restaurant business. He does both very well. Enjoy delicious *kare-kareng baka* (beef and tripe stew) and *pancit* while dining at tables and chairs created by the man and set in a colourful dining room with deep tropical hues. After you've eaten it's a great place to shop and to chat with Ernest who presides over the kitchen.

Tagaytay
Antonio's

A little oasis amongst the pineapple plantations of Tagaytay, this wonderful period mansion and its terraces and gardens have been converted into a renowned eatery by owner and chef Antonio Escalante. You can sit in the covered gazebo or in the open air by the water feature for the perfect candle-lit dining experience.

Antonio's menu changes regularly, taking into account the freshest ingredients, but the restaurant excels in meats, including certified Angus beef, lamb and duck. Every main course has suggested wines to match the food.

Vigan
Grandpa's Inn

An old Spanish mansion-turned-guesthouse and restaurant, this is an excellent and laid-back location to try Vigan *longganisa* and the crunchy *bagnet* pork that are specialities of the region. Locals flock here so the food must be good. The traditional *narra* wood and *capiz* shell architecture takes you back to the era of Spanish rule.

Left: *Dressing up for dinner is optional even at fine restaurants like this one at the Shangri-La, but Filipinos love to put on their best clothes when they are out on the town, to complement the surroundings.*

Surf and Turf

Left: *Rows of* paraws *in full sail wait for clients on White Beach on Boracay.*

Crystal-clear tropical waters, pure white sands and acres of space make a perfect backdrop for a range of leisure activities that have developed around the major resorts and the capital. 'Fun in the sun' could easily be the catch phrase of islands like Boracay, and every large hotel offers a menu of activities should you tire of simply relaxing by the pool. But one sport stands out above all others: diving. The sites here offer the most varied underwater experiences in the world, and some of the most professional dive training.

Over the coming decade the Philippines is also poised to cash in on the massive interest in green activities. The many undeveloped islands and a wild, untamed hinterland are just waiting to be discovered by adrenaline junkies.

Left: Up, up, and away! Rising high under a parasail offers total exhilaration, and great views of the Philippine landscapes and seascapes.

Hiking

The Philippines offers some excellent long- and short-distance walks and hikes through a diverse range of landscapes, and some of its most magnificent and unspoilt corners can only be reached on foot.

Full-on Routes

Experienced hikers will enjoy the challenge of long-distance routes through the tribal lands of the Igorot in the Cordillera, not least those incorporating the breathtaking panoramas of the rice terraces.

Mount Pulag Natural Park has several trails, including the Akiki Trail that takes at least three days to complete. You'll need a guide if you want to reach the summit of Mount Pulag itself. The national park around Mount Guiting-Guiting on Sibuyan Island is one of the richest ecosystems in the Philippines, with a number of rare bird and animal species. The trek to the summit takes at least a full day, but getting there in the first place is just as much an adventure, with only a few boats a week making landfall from Roxas, Lucena or Kalibo.

Exploring Volcanoes

If the idea of climbing an active volcano gets your juices flowing there are several routes to try. The country's most famous spouter, Mount Pinatubo, scene of the last large-scale eruption in 1991, takes two full days to scale and two to descend. You can spend three days on Mount Kanlaon on Negros Island. This 2465m (8088ft) peak has a fresh crater almost 400m (1312ft) deep.

The highest peak on Cebu Island, Mount Osmena, can be climbed in a day, and you can spend about the same length of time on the Taal volcano in the middle of Lake Taal in southern Luzon (though you need to take a boat across Lake Taal to get to the mountain itself).

Be aware that many volcanoes in the Philippines are still active. Always take advice about the activity levels in the area before deciding to go ahead with a walk or trek. The website of the Philippine Institute of Volcanology and Seismology (www.phivolcs.dost.gov.ph) has up-to-date information in English.

Below: Since the eruption of 1991 has ceased, Pinatubo is open once again to walkers and hikers (but do hire a guide).

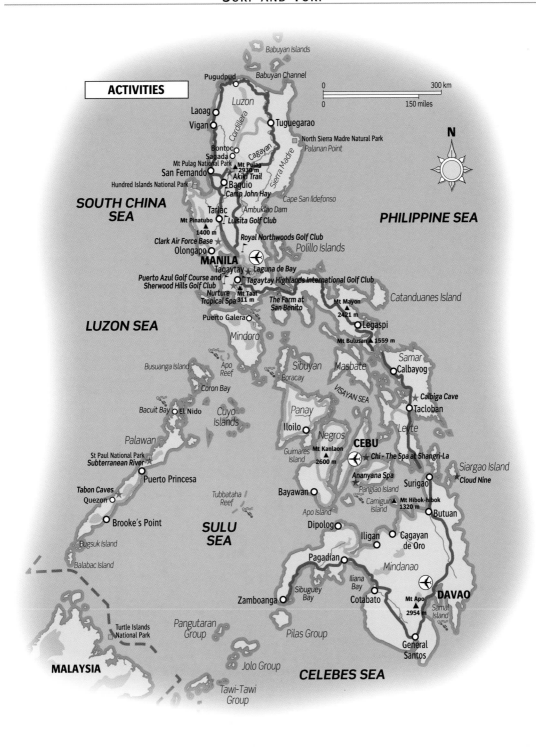

ACTIVITIES

Babuyan Islands

Pugudpud

Babuyan Channel

0   300 km

0   150 miles

Laoag

Luzon

Vigan

Tuguegarao

North Sierra Madre Natural Park

Bontoc

Palanan Point

Sagada

Cordillera

Cagayan

N

Mt Pulag National Park

Mt Pulag 2930 m

San Fernando

Akiki Trail

Sierra Madre

Baguio

Camp John Hay

Cape San Ildefonso

Hundred Islands National Park

SOUTH CHINA SEA

Ambuklao Dam

Tarlac

Mt Pinatubo

Luisita Golf Club

PHILIPPINE SEA

1400 m

Clark Air Force Base

Royal Northwoods Golf Club

Olongapo

MANILA

Polillo Islands

Tagaytay

Laguna de Bay

Puerto Azul Golf Course and Sherwood Hills Golf Club

Tagaytay Highlands International Golf Club

Nurture Tropical Spa

Mt Taat 311 m

The Farm at San Benito

Mt Mayon 2421 m

Catanduanes Island

Puerto Galera

LUZON SEA

Mindoro

Legaspi

Mt Bulusan 1559 m

Busuanga Island

Apo Reef

Sibuyan

Masbate

Samar

Calbayog

Coron Bay

Boracay

VISAYAN SEA

Bacuit Bay

El Nido

Cuyo Islands

Panay

Calbiga Cave

Tacloban

Iloilo

Negros

Leyte

Palawan

Guimaras Island

Mt Kanlaon 2600 m

CEBU

Chi - The Spa at Shangri-La

St Paul National Park
Subterranean River

Siargao Island

Puerto Princesa

Ananyana Spa

Surigao

Cloud Nine

Tabon Caves

Tubbataha Reef

Panglao Island

Quezon

Apo Island

Camiguin Island

Mt Hibok-hibok 1320 m

Butuan

Brooke's Point

SULU SEA

Bayawan

Dipolog

Iligan

Cagayan de Oro

Bugsuk Island

Balabac Island

Pagadian

Mindanao

Zamboanga

Sibuguey Bay

Iliana Bay

Cotabato

DAVAO

Mt Apo 2954 m

Samal Island

MALAYSIA

Turtle Islands National Park

Pangutaran Group

Pilas Group

CELEBES SEA

General Santos

Jolo Group

Tawi-Tawi Group

Shorter Options

There are several routes suited to those with lower fitness levels. From the town of Sagada in the Cordillera you can take hikes of between 20 minutes and an hour to various caves containing ancestral bones. Great views of the rice terraces are your reward for 30-minute to three-hour hikes around Banaue to various signposted panoramic platforms. The two-hour walk to the TayTay Falls in southern Luzon leads through exceptional plantation landscapes.

Before You Start

Whatever your level of experience and fitness, it pays to be well prepared, particularly given the often fierce heat and humidity you'll encounter. Well-fitting, sturdy boots are a must; don't attempt a walk in sandals or flip-flops. Lightweight, full-length trousers and shirt will help stop sunburn; better still, clothing with an SPF rating. Don't forget a hat and sunglasses to top the ensemble. Always carry the following items as a minimum – sun cream, insect repellent and plenty of fresh water. When hiking in the mountains remember it can get very cold and sharp showers can arise quickly. Always equip yourself with warm, protective clothing. Guides are advised at all times.

On Land

Organized land activities are still in the early stages of development, with Filipinos only now realizing that there's business to be made inland. Investments in infrastructure in coming years will push the Philippines onto the radar for sports-minded travellers with specialist interests.

Bird-watching

Almost 200 bird species are endemic to the Philippines and the country has several highly specialized varieties, plus a number that are highly endangered. Add to this a well-documented migratory movement and you'll be able to spot some of the most spectacular birds in Southeast Asia. Many of the national parks make ideal 'twitching' destinations. Touring several different locations during your trip allows you to combine species counts in different ecosystems, latitudes and altitudes.

Mountain Biking

Where two feet dare to tread, two wheels are now just as likely; mountain biking is taking off in the Philippines. The Asian Road Tourism Council funded the first Invitational Mountain Bike Race in Benguet in 2006 and the sport can only continue to grow. So whether it's a week-long enduro-safari or an afternoon at play, here are the locations where you can have some fun.

Using Baguio as a base you can try the trip to the top of 2133m (6998ft) Mount Santo Tomas or head out for the day to the Ambuklao Dam. Sagada and Banaue are surrounded by paths leading though the magnificent rice terraces that also make user-friendly cycle courses (provided you give way to those on foot).

On Cebu you can blaze a trail through stream beds or explore rural lifestyles in the countryside on routes of varying skill levels lasting from a couple of hours to full day – watch out for the burn!

Davao has a well-founded biking scene and Samal Island, just offshore, makes a popular destination. From Davao City you can cycle the trails around Mount Apo for the day. Guimaras Island is also hosting an International Mountain Bike Festival to attract new visitors.

Horse Riding

Despite the long connection with the Spanish and then the Americans, their love of and use of horses is one thing that hasn't transferred to the Philippines and it's not a widely available activity. You can rent horses at the Ananyana Hotel to explore Panglao Island and horses are also available on Boracay. Camp John Hay in Baguio has excellent stables and well-organized bridle paths. They can also provide riding lessons for beginners. There is riding in the Tagaytay Highlands, a series of rolling hills above Lake Taal. The Tagaytay Picnic Grove has stables with animals for rent.

Right: Riding on a banana boat is great fun for all members of the family – young and old can enjoy the crystal-clear waters of the Philippines.

Up, Up and Away

In February each year the old Clark Air Force Base plays host to the Philippines International Hot Air Balloon Fiesta, a celebration of ballooning and flight with participants from over 30 countries. The air is filled with multicoloured envelopes, plus there's a host of powered flight displays, including aerobatic planes, ultra-lights and helicopters.

The Boracay Quintet

Boracay prides itself on being the 'No. 1' resort in the Philippines, and the folks here have invented the ultimate fitness test. Called 'Mambo Number 5', it involves trying your hand at five different activities — boating, windsurfing, trekking, mountain biking and golf. A challenge for energy and skill levels.

River Adventures
Pagsanjan

The only way to get to the spectacular Pagsanjan Falls is by taking a boat trip up the Pagsanjan River that drains into Laguna de Bay. Only a couple of hours from Manila, this is one of the most popular day outings for Filipinos themselves, so you'll be inundated with offers for boat trips — some of them unscrupulous. Pre-booking a trip will save you from being hassled when you arrive.

The trip up-river to the falls takes around 90 minutes as the boatmen tackle a pretty heavy contra-flow of water. The narrowing river gradually enters a curtain of sheer dramatic cliffs, passing many mini-falls until the gorge finally gives up Pagsanjan Falls themselves. Francis Ford Coppola chose this location for the dramatic final scenes of the film *Apocalypse Now*. You can take to a raft if you want to venture under the 10m (33ft) water flow into Devil's Cave. The return journey is a high-speed run down the gorge, now travelling with the flow, and traversing 14 sets of rapids before you return to the boat station. The best times to visit are after the rains have commenced during the wet season (June to October) when water flow is highest and the falls are at their most spectacular.

Above: *A small convoy of canoes makes it way up the Pagsanjan River towards the famous Pagsanjan Falls.*

Bohol

Trips on the Loboc River in the south of Bohol offer a much more stately pace. Large restaurant boats ply the route from Loboc town to the Tontonan Falls, so you can enjoy a long lunch as you travel. The lush banks of the river offer exceptional tropical vistas of *nipa*, banana and coconut palm as you travel along, but one peculiarly Filipino extra is the karaoke on board which, depending on the whim of your fellow passengers, may form a dubious musical serenade to your trip. Smaller motorized canoes can be hired for the same trip if you'd rather miss the communal singsong, or avoid weekends and holidays when Filipino families are at their most numerous.

Palawan

The Subterranean River trip is a must-do when you visit Palawan. Situated north of Puerto Princesa, the river course runs through a karst cave system in the dramatic St Paul mountain range. This is the longest river tunnel yet surveyed and of the 8km (5 miles), 5km (3 miles) are accessible by boat. The journey is an exploration of the surreal shapes emerging in the ever-changing light as you move through the system. Bats and tropical swifts roost in various sub-caves, filling certain sections with high-pitched sound. The contrasting Poyuy-Poyuy River trip follows the mangrove-lined route of the watercourse at its most somnolent.

Action!

If white water is the kind of river adventure you're looking for, head to Kalinga province in the northeast of Luzon, where the Chico and Pinacanauan rivers have now become the new 'Whitewater Rafting Capital'. Trips ranging from six hours to three days lead through magnificent limestone canyons and amongst unspoilt tribal lands surrounded by some of the wildest forested mountainscapes in the country. Cagayan de Oro in northern Mindanao also offers high-adrenaline whitewater rafting, along the Cagayan de Oro River system.

Spas and Wellness

Wellness has become the new buzzword of the early third millennium. No longer do we just want to look good on the outside but we want to feel good on the inside. We've finally understood that 'all work and no play makes Jack a dull boy' but we still need to juggle busy lives at home and at work, so we're searching for ways to recharge our energy levels and pamper ourselves a little.

Massage and other spa treatments have become a popular way of enjoying quality 'me time' and to give tired bodies a much-needed boost. They combine therapies well proven to give relief from the physical symptoms of the stresses of everyday life, with the philosophies practised in many societies in the east and Southeast Asia to offer a more holistic approach to life.

Of course you don't have to jump right on to the whole 'I'm going to change my life forever' bandwagon. Spas and spa treatments are one of the best ways to say thank you to your body and to get away from all the distractions of the day and indulge in sheer pleasure, to let your mind wander and to surrender to the sensuousness of fragrant unguents and therapeutic fingers; perhaps even to be lulled to sleep by the soothing touch of another human hand.

Six of the Best
Chi – The Spa at Shangri-La

This huge complex, ranging over 10,000m² (107,600 sq ft) and surrounded by stone walls, constitutes a city within a city at the Shangri-La Hotel at Mactan. One truly enters paradise as one passes through the portal. Tibetan and Nepalese elements lead the design theme, with the calmness of the Buddha and the simple beauty of the lotus coming to the fore. Plunge pools surrounded by verdant foliage allow bathing and sunning in peace and quiet. Meanwhile, around the perimeter are luxury air-conditioned private treatment villas, each a spacious oasis with its own steam room and a courtyard with bath and open-air treatment areas.

Signature therapies include traditional Himalayan healing massages along with a whole range of more standard therapies. Chi has a specialist water shiatsu (also called watsu) treatment area, a pool with warm water where the therapist manipulates the body as you lie supported by the buoyancy of the liquid.

Ananyana

In contrast to Chi, the spa at Ananyana is diminutive, a beautifully designed single room and private courtyard that provides treatments for singles and couples. Surrounded by fragrant foliage, the soothing sound of a freshwater fountain helps induce total relaxation. A range of massage, aromatherapy and facial treatments are on offer.

Boracay Regency

A sparkling new top-floor spa suite was unveiled at the Boracay Regency in 2007. Sitting high above the bustle of the beachfront, this spacious modern area has several private massage rooms and peaceful balconies where you can relax.

Mandala Spa

This Boracay wellness centre runs yoga courses in addition to having an award-winning day spa. Set inland on some of the highest ground on the island, the spa is surrounded by leafy gardens with day spa villas incorporating traditional Filipino arts and crafts, with luxurious *narra* wood floors and *capiz* shell windows. Mandala Spa offers watsu treatments, plus unique energy rebalancing therapies, in addition to a full range of more mainstream massages and facials.

Nurture Tropical Spa

A wellness resort with an excellent day spa in Tagaytay, where you can simply book one or two treatments or immerse yourself in the total wellness experience. The 2800m^2 (3349-sq-yard) garden includes native *nipa* gazebos, indoor massage rooms and overnight accommodation. The spa offers courses in how to change your life for the day or for years to come.

The Jargon Lexicon

Are you a spa virgin? Then let's try to decipher the standard vocabulary of the industry to help you choose just the right treatment.

- **Acupressure** – Chinese pressure-point massages designed to stimulate the flow of chi energy around the body.
- **Algotherapy** – skin treatments using seaweed.
- **Aromatherapy** – use of essential oils to enhance mood by scenting the air or adding to massage oil for use on the skin. A number of minor conditions such as headaches and sleeplessness can be improved through the use of aromas.
- **Ayurveda** – a whole life system of diet, exercise and treatments to encourage balance within the body.
- **Body wrap** – strips of cotton soaked in creams or oils are wrapped around the body.
- **Botanicals** – extracts of plants.
- **Detox** or **detoxification** – the process of removing toxins (poisons) produced by the body in reaction to things we eat or pollution in the air.
- **Essential oils** – oils extracted from fruits, flowers or other natural sources that impart an aroma when heated. Essential oils are used in aromatherapy and to aid massage.
- **Exfoliation** – removal of the upper layers of the epidermis (skin) to eliminate toxins and promote new cell growth. Various ingredients with a slightly rough texture are mixed with an oil or cream and rubbed over the body to remove dead cells.
- **Hot stone therapy** – warm stones are stroked on the body and placed at certain energy points to improve flow.
- **Hydrotherapy** – underwater jets of water are fired at the body either to sooth muscles, boost circulation or release toxins.
- **Massage** – a mechanical therapy where pressure is applied to the soft tissues to alleviate strains and relax muscles.
- **Paraffin treatment** – warm paraffin is brushed on the body to draw out impurities.
- **Reflexology** – the belief that areas of the feet are linked to areas of the body. Massage of these points promotes improvement in said linked organ.
- **Thalassotherapy** – use of jets of seawater for massage.

Previous page: *The warm tropical air of the Philippines makes massage in the open air a real treat. You can choose from a wealth of western and eastern influenced treatments, and here at San Benito you can also improve your whole being through diet and self-exploration.*

Below: *Your table awaits in serene verdant surroundings at Amanpulo (see page 120), where specially prepared organic ingredients are used in the creams, oils and scrubs. The signature 'Island Indulgence' treatment offers two and a half hours of scrubbing, wrapping and massage to enhance wellbeing and aid relaxation at this jewel of a tropical retreat.*

The Farm at San Benito

The Farm at San Benito does offer a full range of treatments, but it's more of a healing and education centre than a day spa, and it's a great place to come and learn if you are serious about immersing yourself into holistic philosophies about wellness. Staff here work with you on healing principles for mind and body to create balance and vitality.

The resort is set in beautiful tropical gardens with a lake and several soothing fountains. You'll sleep in traditionally styled luxury huts and cottages and enjoy organic vegan food.

Splashing Around

Where tourists congregate, water sports proliferate. The main tourist areas include Boracay Island, Subic Bay north of Manila, Puerto Princesa on Palawan and Puerto Galera on Mindoro. If you don't stay in one of the country's tourist towns, most four- and five-star hotels will have a range of water-sports equipment for you to enjoy (perhaps at extra cost), including one or more of the following:

Kitesurfing

A big growth sport all across the world in the last decade, kitesurfing needs a huge canopy, seemingly miles of cables, a harness and a surfboard. The idea is that one controls the canopy to gain momentum whilst standing on the board. Speed is a goal but so is taking off from and gaining height above the water.

Boracay is the kitesurf capital of the Philippines. You can learn to International Kitesurf Organization (IKO) standards, and Bulabog Beach is kept free of swimmers and boat traffic to allow kitesurfers full rein.

Kayaking

Probably the most widespread water sport option, kayaks make a perfect vehicle for exploring the limpid coastal shallows around myriad Philippine islands and to transport you to jewels of deserted beaches and rocky coves or the inlets of dense mangroves. In benign conditions it only takes a little while to learn the basics and get your balance. The limestone coastline of Palawan is exceptional kayaking country, with its numerous inlets and azure waters. The Big Lagoon and the Small Lagoon

are two of the 'must see' locations on Miniloc Island, Palawan, and the Small Lagoon can only be accessed by kayak or by swimming through the low, narrow entrance.

Windsurfing

The *amihan* wind and shallow waters around Boracay are particularly conducive for windsurfing and the island hosts several competitions on the Pro Asia Tour. Bulabog Beach is the place to be for lessons or for board rental if you are already experienced.

Waterskiing and Wakeboarding

For Filipinos the capital of water sports has to be at Camarines Sur where you'll find the CamSur Watersports Complex, a world-class skiing and wakeboarding (riding on a board while being pulled behind a boat) facility.

Surfing

There are few 'full-on' surfing destinations in the Philippines but those that exist have an excellent reputation amongst aficionados. Siargao Island, off the eastern coast of Mindanao, has excellent breaks along the east coast, including Rock Island and Cloud Nine. The coastline of Ilocos Sur also has a good concentration of breaks around San Fernando City, while Camarines Sur also has several good waves and a handful of surf schools.

Below: What better way to explore the shallow crystal-clear waters around the islands and islets than by kayak? Get away from the rest of the world to explore distant coves and inlets, or find a desert island beach.

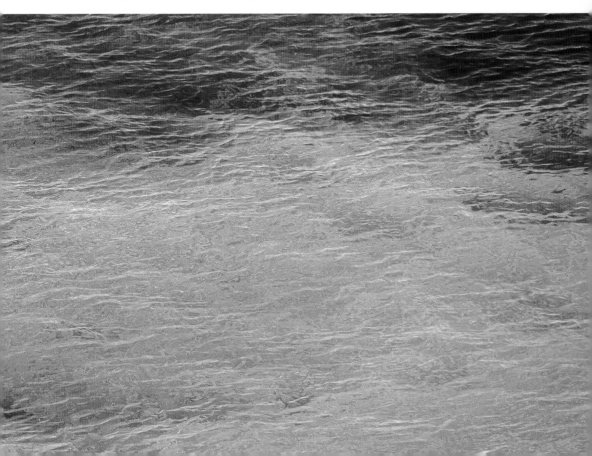

Parascending

Trailing high above the water under a canopy pulled by a boat, parascending isn't only extremely exhilarating but it's a great way to get sensational views of the islands from above. On Boracay you can take in excellent views of both White Beach and Bulabog Beach. The height will give you a totally different perspective on your paradise location.

Jet Ski

These self-drive light motorized vehicles zip across the surface at quite a lick, like a nippy sports car on a track. In most parts of the Philippines, for safety reasons, they are limited to certain sections of water just offshore.

A World Beneath the Waves

The waters of the Philippines have more varied diving opportunities than just about anywhere else in the world. Shallow seas and coastal waters make up much of the country's offshore territory, where more corals proliferate than anywhere else. Over 90% of the world's species are found here, with their attendant coterie of fish and crustaceans. Offshore, and sometimes surprisingly close to the beaches, coral shelves drop suddenly to offer a haven to deeper-dwelling sea creatures, while in certain parts of Philippine national waters ocean trenches are the favourite conduit for larger pelagic marine species that roam the depths or travel long distances on migratory journeys.

The final icing on the cake for Philippine waters makes a plus out of events during the terrible last days of World War II. Several fierce sea battles in the region during 1944 and 1945 produced a rash of shipwrecks that are now open to leisure divers. Many lie in shallow waters making wreck dives possible for even relatively inexperienced divers, though wreck diving is recognized as being more hazardous than reef diving and should only be undertaken with an experienced guide. These wrecks also act as the skeleton for the foundation of new coral reefs as they become slowly integrated into the submarine environment.

You'll find excellent dive centres around the country, often attached to resort hotels. These provide dive training, equipment rental and guides. There's also been a huge growth in 'live-aboard' diving, where you stay on a boat for a few days and the boat travels to various dive sites in a given region. Live-aboard prices include meals and accommodation for the duration of your stay.

A pick of sites around the country include:

Luzon

Anilao, close to Batangas, is the most famous dive resort in the area and a favourite of Manileños who flock from the capital. Offshore, one of the prime sites is Cathedral Rock, now a marine sanctuary. This roofless cavern sits at between 20 and 30 metres (65–98ft) and is only 10 minutes offshore by boat.

Left: Surf's up! At rips around the coastline of the Philippines you'll find local sportsmen mixing with surfers from around the world looking for the next cool place to get out on the board. Hot spots include Siargao Island, Camarines Sur and Ilocos Sur.

North of Manila at Subic Bay there are diving centres on the several wrecks lying in the sheltered waters. *USS New York* was launched in 1891 and served in Philippine waters until she was decommissioned in 1931. The vessel was scuppered in the bay during the initial Japanese invasion to prevent her falling into enemy hands. She lies in 27m (89ft) of water and is now home to barracuda, lionfish and lobster. An earlier wreck, the *San Quentin*, was also scuppered, but this time by the Spanish during the Spanish-American War late in the 19th century.

Mindoro

Puerto Galera has several excellent schools and offers 25 dive sites on the offshore shallows and off neighbouring Verde Island. Sabang Point and beach just offshore has shallow reefs at 7m (23ft) and a couple of wrecks lying at depths shallower than 25m (82ft). The fish here are used to being fed, so they congregate in large numbers.

The most famous sites off Puerto Galera are the shark caves off Escarceo Point where white tips rest in good numbers. Nearby Pink Wall is an outstanding collection of cauliflower corals that is particularly spectacular at night. Currents here do make dive conditions challenging, so take advice before taking to the water.

Apo Reef Marine Natural Park on Mindoro's west coast has an excellent drop-off for wall diving with the chance of diving with large species like shark, rays and tuna. The whole system is over 30km (19 miles) long and the ecosystem offers over 450 documented species of coral. Close by is Hunters Rock, a steep peak with numerous caves and underwater ledges where, once again, large species congregate.

Palawan

Palawan has an exceptional range of differing dive sites with good cave and shelf locations. Off El Nido, the islands of Miniloc, Dilumacad and Matinloc have good variety at relatively shallow depths. Inbogal Point off Matinloc is home to a unique species of angelfish.

There are over 30 wrecks lying in the waters around Busuanga in northern Palawan, following a massive American air strike on the Japanese supply fleet anchored in Coron Bay in September 1944, and 12 of these have been opened up to leisure divers.

Barracuda Lake is an unusual location because one has to climb before it's possible to dive. Limestone peaks surround the lake and it's a 33m (108ft) descent to the

entrance of a collapsed cave. Another cave dive, Cathedral Cave (around Basuanga island) has spectacular illumination thanks to a fissure in the ceiling. There is exciting diving with varied sea life to a depth of 12m (39ft).

The Visayas

There are dive sites just off from Boracay's amazing White Beach, but one of the most dramatic is Tapak, off the northern tip, where reef walls descend from 30m (98ft) to 60m (197ft) and offer a great variety of soft corals along with fish of all sizes, including hammerhead sharks and manta rays. Sea conditions can be tricky here, however, so the conditions only suit experienced divers.

The shallow reefs of Panglao Island, Bohol, make interesting diving possible practically from the beach around Alona, though Pamilacan Island, which means 'resting place of the mantas', is famed for just that reason. Cervera Shoal is known for its colony of sea snakes, as well as pelagic species such as sharks.

Apo Island, off the south coast of Negros (not to be confused with Apo Reef), offers one of the best all-round sites in the Philippines for its range of corals, tropical fish species and large pelagics, including barracuda and sharks.

Mindanao and the Sulu Sea

Several sites lie around Samal Island, within easy reach of Davao, which has a developing tourist infrastructure. Marissa 1, 2 and 3 have reefs that max out at 30m (98ft). Here there'll be a good chance of spotting hawksbill turtles surveying the area.

Tubbataha Reefs offshore are a prime 'live-aboard' site. These archetypal Pacific reefs form a vast field of shallow plateau formations, caves and ledges, plus pristine tiny islets. The corals here are spectacular but this is also a breeding ground for many fish species.

Right: Philippine reefs are some of the most abundant on the planet, with myriad species of tropical fish including these playful Moorish Idols grazing close to the coral bed. Corals thrive best in warm shallow seas such as those that proliferate around the archipelago.

Take a Boat Trip

Bangkas are the transport of choice for fishermen and when locals make short inter-island trips. You can hire a *bangka* to take you off to a remote beach for the day, or to do a spot of fishing or snorkelling. For a romantic end to the day, head out west to watch the sun slip below the horizon.

Hundred Islands National Park

Set in horseshoe-shaped Lingayen Gulf, the hundred-plus islands in the Hundred Islands National Park are some of the country's lesser-known playgrounds, having few large international hotels. A boat trip can include visits to limestone caves, deserted islets with stunning beaches, beach restaurants with tropical views and a million places to swim and snorkel.

Lake Taal

Of the 22 active volcanoes in the Philippines, Taal is probably the most picturesque, surrounded as it is by the dark tranquil waters of its eponymous lake. A rare 'lake within a volcano within a lake within a volcano', Lake Taal occupies a vast caldera created by an ancient eruption of its volcano. But re-emerging from the heart

of the lake, 'baby Taal' volcano cone slowly grows, with another tiny lake at its centre. You can take *bangka* trips from the northern coast of Lake Taal to the inner crater, being dropped off at a jetty at Buco to explore the landscape of the active cone.

Laguna de Bay

This huge shallow body of water covers a vast area of Luzon to the southeast of Manila and it is home to a fishing community that live in stilted bamboo huts out on the water. The families eke a living here, but their lifestyle is fascinating. Boat trips are not as well organ-

Whale Watching

Many of the large pelagic marine species make their way through Philippine waters, using the channels between the islands as conduits. An increasing number of Filipino fishermen are now catering to tourists who want to spot these animals, rather than catching them on hooks or in nets. Dolphins are the most numerous of the species but it's also possible to see whale sharks, melon-headed whales, pilot whales and pygmy sperm and blue whales. The best time to see them is between February and June and the best locations are around Pamilacan off Bohol, off Donsol in southern Luzon and Bais City in Negros Oriental.

ized as at Lake Taal, but you are sure to meet a boatman who is willing to take you for a tour around and perhaps introduce you to his family (if you visit a cottage, leave a small gratuity).

Corregidor

The tiny island of Corregidor at the mouth of Manila Bay is inextricably linked with World War II. The island was the headquarters of General MacArthur's American/Filipino forces until he was evacuated from the island in 1942. There was bloody fighting again in 1945 when the Americans retook Corregidor. Today, remains of the military outposts are a poignant reminder of the combat, including the Malinta tunnel complex, a subterranean military headquarters complete with hospital that was built into Mount Malinta in the late 1920s.

Tour boats for trips to Corregidor depart from the pier close to the Cultural Center of the Philippines on the waterfront in Manila at 08:00 and the journey takes one hour.

Left: Large bangkas *make roomy and comfortable ferry boats, disgorging their passengers directly onto the soft sandy beach, such as here at Dimakya Island off Coron, for a day of fun in the sun.*

Caving and Spelunking

It's fair to say that the landscape of the Philippines is like a Swiss cheese, riddled with holes, and some of immense size and complexity. In tribal communities caves took on a supernatural aura. Their much-revered ancestors were buried in caves in the Cordillera, from where they would cast a benevolent eye over ensuing rice harvests.

Several large cave complexes have been discovered around the islands in the last 100 years and some have even developed into tourist attractions, but it's only been in the last 15 years that caves have caught the eye of adventure-sports enthusiasts, and caving or spelunking is a big growth area. Whether you choose to be a passive or active cave explorer, it's an element of the environment that shouldn't be ignored.

Spelunking?

This unusual word, from the Latin *spelunca* (cave), simply describes the activity of exploring caves, either on foot or with the help of ropes or underwater breathing apparatus.

Where to Go
The Big One

The largest single cave system in the country, indeed one of the largest in Asia, so far discovered and documented is Calbiga Cave on Samar Island. Measured at almost 3000 hectares (7413 acres) in area by the Italian team that surveyed it, the complex comprises 12 connected caverns and includes a subterranean river.

Some of the Best of the Rest

The Peñablanca region of the Northern Sierra Madre Natural Park in Northern Luzon has over 300 caves, of which only 75 have been documented, but these form the basis of some excellent spelunking. Odessa has 8km (5 miles) of passages and is the largest complex in the region. Callao Caves are some of the major tourist attractions in the park, accessed by steps – almost 200 of them. Several caves are illuminated

Above: *Cave exploration, or spelunking, is a new and growing sport in the Philippines. Easily accessible caves need no experience or specialist equipment and clothing, but care is needed on entry and exit.*

for non-sports people to explore. One of them has a chapel inside.

The landscape around Sagada, also in northern Luzon, has 60 caves with underground streams and pools, plus exceptional stalactites and stalagmites. Sumaging Cave is the largest and doesn't require any special skills to explore.

Cebu has plenty to offer. Lantoy Cave system in Argao Lantoy National Park is a truly monumental system with a final rappel of 25m (82ft) down a waterfall. The Barili Caves are a huge network, and were used by locals to escape the clutches of the Japanese during World War II. Sections here are suitable for spelunking beginners.

Tabon Caves in southern Palawan have yielded huge amounts of information about the lives of the earliest Filipinos. The complex covers a vast area around Lipuun Point, with over 200 individual caverns and niches, but only one is open to the public. You must take a guide when you visit and these can be arranged at the Palawan Museum in Quezon.

Less-explored caves may suit experienced spelunkers with their own equipment. Bulabog Puti-An National Park, in the heart of Panay Island, has a complex of almost 40 caves and there are several caves in the centre of Siquijor Island, the best known of which is Cantabon Cave. However, it's fair to say that the Philippines has many caves that have never been explored.

Casinos and Gambling

Filipinos enjoy gambling, though for most the frenzy and excitement centres around *sabong* (cock fighting) rather than the gaming tables. Hundreds of thousands of pesos change hands every day at the *sabungan* (arena) and some fights are real high stakes. Note that gambling within the arena is still controlled without the use of computers and other electronic devices or written tabs. Gamblers in the crowd signal to the bookies with a complicated set of hand gestures conveying which bird and how much. Betting can take place pretty much up until the animals are let loose in the ring.

Below: Making a bet is a popular pastime in the Philippines, be it at the gaming tables, the track or at the cock-fighting ring. The average bet is small, but high rollers can still be found in the casinos.

In Metro Manila (the greater city district) there are two casinos attached to hotels – the Heritage Hotel in Pasay City, and the Hyatt Hotel in Malate.

Waterfront Hotels has two properties in Cebu City that have casinos. The Waterfront Cebu City is close to the downtown area and offers baccarat, blackjack and roulette, while the Waterfront Airport is on Mactan Island and offers craps, stud poker and pontoon in addition to the table games. Casino Filipino Tagaytay in Tagaytay offers blackjack, craps, baccarat, poker and even bingo.

Fort Ilocandia Hotel near Laoag was built by the Marcoses for their daughter Irene's wedding in 1983. The casino is the largest in the Philippines, with six differently designed gambling salons.

Fontana Casino is part of the Fontana Leisure Parks complex at Clark Field in Pampanga, with a 2000m² (21,520-sq-ft) gaming room and helicopter transfers from Manila direct to the door.

Santa Ana Park is home to the Philippine Racing Club which operates a card of races throughout the year. Total betting at the track and in off-track betting stations has topped three billion pesos annually since the start of the millennium.

Golf

The Philippines has yet to see the investment in resort-based golf that has taken place in other countries of Southeast Asia, but there are still more than enough courses where addicts can keep that swing in peak condition. Courses tend to be concentrated within easy travelling distance of Manila. Here is a list of the best.

Perhaps the most unusual course in the country is the Intramuros Golf Club, whose greens wrap the old city walls. Stray balls sometime find themselves breaking windows in the old town.

Right: The golf course at Intramuros features ranging holes set in the shadow of the old walled city in the heart of downtown Manila. In the background is the neoclassical former Congress Building, now the National Museum.

Camp John Hay in Baguio was used by the American military for their R&R. The golf course has recently been renovated by Jack Nicklaus and has narrow fairways and sloping greens that punish overconfident play.

Fairways and Bluewater Resort Golf and Country Club has a 5517m (6034-yard) par 72 18-hole course and is the only course on Boracay.

Luisita Golf Club in Tarlac was designed by Robert Trent-Jones and is considered the toughest in the country.

Puerto Azul Golf Course in Ternate, Cavite, makes it into the 'Top 100 courses outside the USA' list in *Golf Digest*, sitting pretty at number 58.

Royal Northwoods Golf Club at San Rafael in Bulacan is a Graham Marsh designed course.

Sherwood Hills Golf Club in Cavite is the second Philippine course in the 'Top 100 courses outside the USA' according to *Golf Digest*, resting at number 85.

Tagaytay Highlands International Golf Club sits high above Lake Taal and is accessible by a cable car. Man-made lakes are a feature of the course.

The aptly named Wack Wack Golf Club in Mandaluyong City, Manila, plays host to the annual Philippine Open tournament, an official event on the Asia Tour.

Travel Directory

Left: Bangka *outrigger boats bob in the azure shallows off Snake Island, El Nido, Bacuit Bay, Palawan – one of a million pleasing views around the islands of the Philippines.*

The Travel Directory gives you all the information you need to make the most of your trip to the Philippines.

Practical guidelines are designed to help you plan your visit, with tips on how and when to travel, including contact details of airlines and where to find tourist information. You'll find helpful facts about Philippine currency, national holidays and climate, along with pointers on what to pack and how to get around. We've included addresses, telephone numbers and websites for all the featured hotels and restaurants, plus a few more for travellers with different budgets. There are also comprehensive details of all the organizations, attractions and museums mentioned in the text.

Left: A rustic wooden jetty is your starting point for adventures on the water or underneath the waves at El Nido resort in Bacuit Bay.

Practical Guide
Tourist Information

The Department of Tourism is the official body responsible for visitor information. They can be contacted at their head office: T.M. Kalaw Street, Rizal Park, P.O. Box 31451, Manila, tel: 2 599 031, www.tourism.gov.ph

There are official tourist offices in Manila, San Fernando (La Union), San Fernando (Pampanga), Baguio, Laoag, Tuguegareo, Legazpi, Iloilo, Boracay, Bacolod, Lau-Lapu City, Tacloban, Zamboanga, Cagayan de Oro, Davao, Cotabato and Batuan.

The authority operates agencies in the following countries – UK, Germany, China, Singapore, USA, Australia, Korea, Japan, Taiwan and Hong Kong.

Entry Requirements

All visitors must be in possession of a valid passport with at least six months to run at the end of their stay. They must also have a return air ticket and, if asked, be able to prove that they have sufficient funds to finance their stay.

Officials will initially grant entry on a visitor's visa for up to 21 days. Visas can be extended for another 38 days if you purchase a visa extension through the Bureau of Immigration. The main office is at Magallenes Drive, Intramuros, Manila, tel: 2 527 3260.

You'll need a copy of the information page of your passport and the applicable fee (currently 2020 pesos). Take onward flight details with you if you have them. You may need to provide proof that you can support yourself during your extension.

If you overstay the initial 21-day visa and you don't get a visa extension, you'll be fined as you leave the country (by the immigration officer). This covers the 2020 pesos you should have paid, plus a fine of 500 pesos and an express fee of 500 pesos for immediate processing.

Customs

Passengers over the age of 18 can import the following items duty-free:
- 400 cigarettes or 2 tins of tobacco
- 2 bottles of wine or spirits (no more than 1 litre each)

All ports and airports charge a government collection departure tax ranging from 750 pesos for international departures from Manila to 20 pesos from ports like Tagbilaran.

Under current security guidelines NO liquids will be allowed into the departure lounges or onto flights to and from Manila – not even the 100ml allowed at other airports in other countries.

Arriving (Air Travel)

Manila's Ninoy Aquino International Airport is the main port of entry. The terminal is modern and air conditioned with arrival duty-free, banks, ATMs, car rental agency offices and taxi office.

The second international port of entry is Cebu City which is smaller with fewer facilities though there are banks, ATMs and car rental agency offices.

There are no direct flights from Europe to the Philippines. Passengers can use any one of the major Southeast Asian hubs – Bangkok, Hong Kong, Singapore or Kuala Lumpur – or Dubai as a gateway, with onward flights by Philippines Airlines (www.philippines airlines.com). Philippines Airlines also flies to Tokyo, Taipei, Vancouver, Los Angeles, Las Vegas, Honolulu, Sydney and Melbourne, plus a range of other cities around Indo-China (a total of 31 international destinations). Low-cost airline Cebu Pacific (www.cebu pacificair.com) flies from Bangkok, Hong Kong, Kuala Lumpur and Singapore to Manila or Cebu. Thai Airways (www.thaiair.com) and Singapore Airlines (www. singaporeair.com) also fly to Manila.

Unless one of these airlines has a special fare deal at the time of your trip, the keenest price competition is to be found with Internet travel shops such as Expedia (www.expedia.com) or Opodo (www.opodo.com).

Roads and Driving
General Guidelines

Driving is on the right-hand side of the highway with overtaking on the left. Most roads are two lane and many are narrow with no pedestrian walkway, so you'll encounter people and dogs walking on the road shoulders. Traffic is controlled by traffic lights but at peak times may be controlled by police officers. On many

Above: Philippines Airlines is the country's national carrier and the longest operating airline in Southeast Asia.

routes in towns and villages traffic is controlled by speed bumps. These may or may not be indicated beforehand. Be aware that driving is hazardous. In cities, especially Manila, roads are gridlocked with traffic, while on rural roads speed will be dictated by the slowest moving vehicle. This may be a cart pulled by a water buffalo or a motorcycle taxi whose maximum speed is 25kph (15mph).

Speed Limits
• On crowded streets, in school zones and when passing stationary vehicles: 30kph (18mph)
• Through streets or boulevards: 40kph (24mph)
• Open roads (no blind bends): 80kph (49mph)
• On other city streets: 30kph (18mph)

Parking
This is difficult in most large towns.

Fuel
All main towns have fuel stations, generally open Mon–Sat 09:00–19:00.

Car Rental
It's possible to rent a car at the airport on your arrival or to pick up the vehicle at your hotel. Many rental companies will travel to your hotel to deliver a vehicle. Major companies such as Avis, Europcar and Hertz are established here but you may get a more competitive rate with a local company.

A full national or an international driving licence will be needed for rental. Minimum age for rental is 21 with a full licence for at least one year (some companies have a minimum age requirement of 25 for some vehicles).

Always carry your driver's licence and rental document when you drive the vehicle.

Buses and Taxis
Taxis make an excellent form of transport both for single journeys and for sightseeing. The fleet has been modernized in recent years and offers comfortable and reliable vehicles. Journeys are supposed to be metered but these are rarely used, so agree a price beforehand (ask your hotel reception for a guide price). Taxi drivers are also happy to agree a set price for a morning, day or few days sightseeing so you don't have the worry of navigating around the island. Again, agree a price beforehand.

The bus network on Luzon and Mindanao is comprehensive, but journeys may be long and uncomfortable, with many buses being old and not well maintained, and the timetables may not be ideal for sightseeing. You can find local timetables at all bus depots or stations.

Clothes (What to Pack)

Most of the year, the tropical climate of the Philippines is ideal for light, loose clothing – shorts, T-shirts, short-sleeved shirts and summer dresses. Light long-sleeved shirts and light full-length trousers are advisable cover-ups in case of too much sun exposure. Clothing with an SPF factor is ideal.

Note that Filipinos are generally conservative dressers and beachwear should not be worn anywhere else but at the beach.

In the mountains around Baguio it can feel chilly in the early morning or the evenings, so a light sweater or fleece would be a useful addition when sightseeing or hiking.

You'll need to be properly dressed to enter churches and mosques. Cover shoulders and knees and leave shoes at the entrance to mosques. Take hats off when entering churches but women may need to cover their heads when entering mosques.

Money Matters
Currency

The currency is the peso (Piso in Pilipino) denoted as P or a P with a horizontal line through the top. Each peso is divided into 100 *centavos*. Banknotes come in denominations of P10, P20, P50, P100, P200, P500 and P1000, and coins in 5c, 10c, 25c, P1, P5, P10.

Currency Exchange

You can exchange foreign currency at banks and most hotels will also offer a service, though they may charge a fee or offer a less favourable exchange rate.

Traveller's Cheques

These are the safest way to carry holiday cash as they can be replaced if they are lost or stolen. But the exchange rate may not be favourable. You can change these at hotels and banks.

ATMs

ATMs are becoming more numerous and you will certainly be able to get cash in the major towns with a Cirrus card or credit card as long as you have a Personal Identification Number (PIN). If you intend to travel in rural areas, take a supply of pesos.

Credit Cards

Credit cards are accepted in the major resorts in the Philippines. The most popular are MasterCard and Visa. However, smaller enterprises work on a cash-only basis.

Banking Hours

Opening hours are Mon–Fri 09:00–15:00.

Taxes

The Philippines government applies a 10% Value Added Tax on many goods and services. This will be included in the final price.

Tipping

Tipping is expected in the Philippines. Some hotels and restaurants automatically add a service charge to the bill. Be sure to clarify whether prices include service. Otherwise 10% is a standard tip.

Trading Hours
Shops

Shopping hours are generally Mon–Sat 10:00–20:00 though some malls stay open till 21:00.

Offices

In the public sector businesses are open Mon–Fri 08:00–17:00 or 09:00–18:00, though some private enterprises stay open until 20:00.

Post Offices

Opening hours are Mon–Fri 08:00–17:00.

Churches

Some churches may close during lunchtime and early afternoon.

Telephones

General Information

The Philippines has a modern telephone system in the major urban areas, with several telecom companies, including Philippine Long Distance Telecom Company (PLDT), Globetelecom and Digital Telecommunications Philippines. All hotels have International Direct Dialling for international calls but will charge a premium for this service. Check prices before making your call to avoid an unexpected charge.

Public Phones

Public phones can only be used for local calls.

Mobile Phones

Globetelecom, Digital Telecommunications Philippines and Smart all have coverage of the populated areas, with partnership agreements with major foreign telecom companies. Check with your own mobile provider about continuation of service before departing for the Philippines. The country should be up for an award as the texting capital of the world – this was a free service when it was first introduced and everyone has become addicted.

Calling the Philippines

The international calling code for the Philippines is 63. Local codes may have two or three digits. Domestic directory enquiries with PLDT, tel: 0800 890 063.

Calling Home

To make an international call from the Philippines dial 00 followed by the country code (UK 44, France 33, Australia 61, NZ 64, USA and Canada 1, South Africa 27).

Crime

The urban areas of the Philippines have a problem with petty crime. If you visit Manila stay in the main tourist areas and modern cities such as Makati and always ask advice if you intend to walk anywhere. Only use official taxis when you choose to travel by taxi. Don't wear flashy jewellery or carry expensive electronic goods if you travel by public transport.

Pickpockets operate in crowded areas such as markets so keep cash and passports in a secure place. Bags should be held close to the body with straps across the chest.

Do not leave valuables in a car and leave nothing at all on show.

Do not carry large amounts of cash or valuables with you.

Deposit valuables in the hotel safes.

Take extra care at cash-point machines – don't allow bystanders to see your PIN or grab your cash.

Put all money away before you leave banks or bureau de change kiosks.

Don't leave valuables unattended in cafés or restaurants, or on the beach.

Electricity

220 volt with a mixture of British-style three-pin and European-style two-pin plugs. Most hotels have 110-volt outlets.

Embassies

British Embassy

Floors 15–17, LV Locsin Building
6752 Ayala Avenue
1226 Makati
Metro Manila
tel: 2 580 8700
Also, Honorary Consuls in Angeles City, Cebu and Olongapo

US Embassy

1201 Roxas Boulevard
Ermita 1000
Manila
tel: 2 528 6300
Also, Consulate in Davao

Australian High Commission

Level 23, Tower 2 RCBC Plaza
6819 Ayala Avenue
Makati, Metro Manila
tel: 2 757 8100

Canadian Embassy

Levels 6–8, Tower 2 RCBC Plaza
6819 Ayala Avenue
Makati, Metro Manila
tel: 2 857 9000

Republic of Ireland

Honorary Consul
70 Jupiter Street, Bel Air 1
Makati, Metro Manila
tel: 2 896 4668

New Zealand

23rd Floor, BPI Buendia Center
Sen Gil Puyat Avenue
Makati, Metro Manila
tel: 2 891 5358

South Africa

29th Floor, Yuchengco Tower
RCBC Plaza
6819 Ayala Avenue
Makati, Metro Manila
tel: 2 899 9383

Emergencies

The emergency numbers are:
Police: 117
Fire services: There is no national number for the fire services.
Ambulance (SAMU): There is no national ambulance service in the country. Ambulances are called via the police, attending physician or by calling direct to the local hospital.

Health

The Philippines is a tropical country with high temperatures and humidity. Infections start easily in these conditions, so make sure that any small cuts or grazes, etc. are thoroughly cleaned and covered.

Vaccinations

No vaccinations are required to enter the Philippines.

However, a yellow fever vaccination certificate will need to be shown for those travelling from an infected area.

Water

Always drink bottled water or carry purifying tablets if you are unsure of the water supply. Also beware of the source of any ice you have in drinks. Hotels have safe supplies but in the countryside this may not be the case. Avoid ice in drinks (and ice cream) where you are unsure of the source.

Health Hazards

Malaria is endemic to certain parts of the country and it's important that you get advice from your doctor regarding effective prevention. Your Hepatitis A prevention should be up to date for your trip.

The risk of encountering other unpleasant and dangerous diseases depends on where you intend to stay and what you intend to do. If you plan to explore the mountain areas and spend time (more than a month), you'll need to think about protection against typhoid, Hepatitis B, meningococcus and Japanese encephalitis.

Mosquito-bite prevention will aid against the risk of malaria but also lesser-known diseases like chikungunya and dengue fever.

Most other holiday 'nasties' are preventable and are generally the result of the hot climate. Limit your time in the sun, particularly in the early phase of your trip, to avoid sunburn. Drink plenty of fluids (but limit alcohol intake) to avoid dehydration. Make sure that street food is properly cooked.

Animal Hazards

The Philippines has several species of poisonous or dangerous animals. Poisonous snakes include cobras and vipers but these are confined to less-populated areas.

Be aware, however, that one of the most dangerous animals in Southeast Asia is the water buffalo. They may seem docile but they can be very unpredictable.

There are also dangers in the water. Several areas have populations of sea snakes. Swim away if you see one in the water. Box jellyfish are found in the waters between October and May. Both stonefish and lionfish have venomous barbs and should never be touched. Avoid stepping on or touching sea urchins as the spines can break off and become embedded in your skin. It's recommended that you wear rubber shoes when swimming to avoid accidental penetration.

The Philippines has many dogs which, although generally docile, should never be petted as they may carry rabies, have ticks and other parasites, and any bites may become infected.

Medical Services

All large towns and cities have adequate public hospital facilities, but cities also have private hospitals where, although prices are more expensive, care is considered to be more comprehensive.

In rural areas and on small remote islands, it's impossible to find comprehensive health care. Your hotel will have the telephone number of a doctor on call. If you are in need of emergency treatment you will need to be transferred to a bigger town or city and this can be expensive. Carry adequate insurance to cover injury or illness whilst on your trip.

Manila
Makati Medical Center
Amorsolo Street
Makati
tel: 2 815 9911
Baguio
St Louis Hospital of the Sacred Heart
2600 Baguio
tel: 074 442 7606
Cagayan de Oro
Northern Mindanao Medical Center
Capital Compound
tel: 88 856 5490

Language

Most Filipinos are bi- or trilingual, speaking English, Pilipino and perhaps another indigenous language depending on their background. In restaurants and hotels both languages will be spoken fluently. The street language, however, will depend on exactly where you are.

Pilipino has addresses in formal and informal style. In dealing with people, it's courteous to use the formal until invited to do otherwise. Women should be referred to as 'Missus' or 'Miss', while men should be referred to as 'mama'.

You'll notice that you'll be treated with courtesy in shops, hotels and restaurants with staff using 'sir' or 'madam' as a matter of course. If you have any official dealings, such as organizing a visa extension, use of the appropriate 'sir' or 'madam' smoothes the way.

Public Holidays

1 January – New Year celebrations
24 February – EDSA Revolution Day
9 April – Araw ng Kagitingan (Day of Valor or Bataan Day)
1 May – Labour Day
12 June – Independence Day
Last Sunday in August – National Heroes' Day
1 November – All Saints' Day (Christian)
30 November – Bonifacio Day
25 December – Christmas Day (Christian)
30 December – Rizal Day

Moveable Dates

Maundy Thursday (Christian)
Good Friday (Christian)
Eid-El-Fitr (Muslim)
Eid-El-Adha (Muslim)

Time

The Philippines is 8 hours ahead of Greenwich Mean Time.

Books

Dive Guide: The Philippines by Jack Jackson (ISBN 1845376293) – comprehensive information for divers.
Birds of The Philippines (A Photographic Guide) by Tim Fisher and Nigel Hicks (ISBN: 1859745105) – a companion for bird-watchers.
Manila My Manila by Nick Joaquin (ISBN 971-569-313-X) – a popular history of the city written by one of its own sons.

Contact Details
Hotels

Amanpulo (*see* page 120)
Pamalican Island
Cuyo Islands
tel: 2 759 4040
fax: 2 759 4044
www.amanresorts.com

Ananyana (*see* page 117)
Doljo Beach
Panglao Island
Bohol
tel: 38 503 8101
www.ananyana.com

Boracay Regency Beach Resort
(*see* page 114)
Station 2
Balabag
Boracay
tel: 36 288 6111
fax: 36 288 6777
www.boracayregency.com

Club Paradise
(*see* page 115)
Dimakya Island
Coron
Palawan
tel: 2 838 4956
fax: 2 838 4462
www.clubparadisepalawan.com

Country Suites
300 Calamba Road
San José
Tagaytay City
tel: 46 413 4567
fax: 46 416 1076
www.discoverycountrysuites.com
This modern mansion on the crater
of Lake Taal has been converted

into a small, tasteful boutique
hotel with plunge pool and
excellent restaurant.

Discovery Shores
(*see* page 113)
Station 1 Balabag
Boracay
tel: 36 288 4500
fax: 36 288 4505
www.discoveryshoresboracay.com

Discovery Suites
25 ADB Avenue
Ortigas Center
Pasig City, Manila
tel: 2 683 8222
fax: 2 683 8333
www.discoverysuites.com
A modern suite hotel in the heart
of the Pasig shopping district.
There's a good gym and small
indoor pool, a lounge and gourmet
restaurant.

El Nido Resorts Lagen Island
(*see* page 112)
Lagen Island, Palawan
tel: 2 759 4050
10 Knots Development Corporation
(Management Company)
tel: 2 894 5644
fax: 2 810 3620
Island Voyager: 2 851 5670
www.elnidoresorts.com

The Manor (*see* page 105)
Camp John Hay
Loakan Road
Baguio
tel: 74 446 0231
fax: 74 445 0420
www.campjohnhayhotels.com

Pansukian Resort
(*see* page 108)
Barangay Malinao
Siargao Island
Surigao del Norte
tel: 920 901 2072
www.pansukian.com

**Shangri-La Mactan Island
Resort & Spa**
(*see* page 106)
Punta Engaño Road
Lapu-Lapu City
Mactan Island, Cebu
tel: 32 231 0288
fax: 32 231 1688
www.shangri-la.com

Sitio Remedios
Barangay Currimao
Ilocos Norte
tel: 0917 322 0217
www.sitioremedios.com
A dozen traditional Ilocano houses
have been rescued, renovated and
set in a beachfront courtyard at
this peaceful north Luzon retreat.
This is a labour of love for the
owner – neurosurgeon and art
lover Jovan Cuanang.

Spider House
Diniwid Beach, Boracay
tel: 36 288 3833
Simple *nipa* shacks built into the
rocky crevice of the bay next to
White Beach. Spectacular views
but no mod cons.

The Peninsula (*see* page 104)
Corner of Ayala and Makati Avenues
1226 Makati City, Metro Manila
tel: 2 231 0288

fax: 2 815 4825
www.peninsula.com

Restaurants
83 Gallery Cafe
83 Rizal Street, Pagsanjan
tel: 49 808 0034
Open daily 11:00–22:00

Abaca (*see* page 144)
Punta Engaño
Mactan Island, Cebu
tel: 63 324 958456
www.abacaresort.com
Open Tue–Sun 17:30–22:30
Reservations recommended

Abé (*see* page 144)
Serendra Circle
Fort Bonifacio, Manila
tel: 2 856 0526
Open daily 12:00–14:00,
18:00–23:00
Reservations recommended

Antonio's (*see* page 147)
Barangay Neogan (signposted from
the main Tagaytay road)
Tagaytay
tel: 63917 899 2866
Open Wed–Sun 11:30–13:30,
Tue–Sun 17:30–19:30

Apartment 1B (*see* page 144)
Ground Floor, One Lafayette
Square
143 L.P. Leviste Corner
Sedeno Street
Salcedo Village
Makati City
tel: 843 4075
Open Mon–Thu 07:00–23:00,
Fri–Sat 07:00–02:00

Bamboo Lounge (*see* page 146)
On the beach
Station 1, Boracay
tel: 036 288 3161
Open 24 hours

Café by the Ruins (*see* page 144)
25 Chuntung Street
Baguio
tel: 74 442 4010
Open daily 08:00–21:00

Cowrie Cove (*see* page 145)
Shangri-La's Mactan Island Resort
and Spa
Punta Engaño Road
Lapu-Lapu City
Mactan Island
Cebu
tel: 32 231 0288
Open daily 18:00–22:00

Dos Mestizos (*see* page 147)
Wonderland St
Manggayad Barangay
Manoc-Manoc
Boracay
tel: 036 288 6789
Open daily 11:00–00:00

Grandpa's Inn (*see* page 147)
1 Bonifacio St
Vigan
tel: 077 722 2118
Open daily 07:00–10:00,
12:00–15:00, 18:00–22:00

Le Chef at the Manor
(*see* page 144)
Manor Hotel
Camp John Hay
Loakan Road
Baguio

tel: 74 446 0231
Open daily 06:30–22:00

M Café (*see* page 144)
Ayala Museum
Greenbelt Mall
Makati Avenue (corner of de la
Rosa Street)
Makati, Metro Manila
tel: 2 757 3000
Open 06:30–23:00

Transport
Philippines Airlines
Legazpi Street
Legazpi Village
Makati
Metro Manila
tel: 2 818 0111
www.philippineairlines.com

Cebu Pacific Airlines
16th Floor
Equitable PCI Tower
San Miguel Avenue
Pasig City
Manila
tel: 800 1888 2582 (toll free in
the Philippines) or 2 638 1746
www.cebupacificair.com

Seair
Second floor
Dona Concepcion Building
Arniaz Avenue
Makati
Metro Manila
tel: 2 849 0100
www.flyseair.com

Cathay Pacific
22nd floor
LKG Tower

6801 Ayala Avenue
Makati
Metro Manila
tel: 2 757 0888
www.cathaypacific.com

Thai Airways
Country Space 1 Building
Sen Gil J. Puyat Avenue
Makati
Metro Manila
tel: 2 834 0366
www.thaiair.com

Asian Spirit
G4 BSA Towers
108 Legazpi Street
Makati, Metro Manila
tel: 2 855 3333
www.asianspirit.com

Superferries
12th Floor
Times Plaza Building
United Nations Avenue
Manila
tel: 2 528 7979

Attractions
American War Cemetery
(*see* page 57)
Global City
Taguig, Manila
Open daily 09:00–17:00

Bell Church (*see* page 70)
Off the La Trinidad Road
Baguio
Open daily 06:00–17:00

Calauit Game Reserve and Wildlife Sanctuary (*see* page 37)
Calauit Island, off Busuanga

Open daily 07:00–17:30

Casa Manila (*see* page 63)
Plaza San Luis Complex
Corner Callé General Luna and
Callé Real
tel: 2 527 4084
Open Tue–Sun 09:00–18:00

Casa Gorordo (*see* page 63)
5 Calle Lopez Jeana
Cebu City
tel: 32 255 5630
Open Tue–Sun 09:00–12:00,
13:00–17:30

Casa Rocha-Suarez Heritage Center
Galle Franklin 3
Tagbilaran
Bohol
tel: 38 411 5933
Open: ring for hours

Center for Philippine Raptors
Makiling Botanical Gardens
Los Baños
Laguna de Bay
tel: 49 536 2637
Open daily 08:00–17:00

Chocolate Hills (*see* page 34)
Carmen, Bohol
Open 24 hours

Church of the Immaculate Conception (San Augustin) and Museum (*see* page 93)
Callé General Luna
Intramuros, Manila
tel: 2 527 4060
Open daily 09:00–12:00,
13:00–16:00

Clarin Ancestral Home
(*see* page 63)
Laoy, Bohol
Open daily 08:00–17:30

Cultural Center of the Philippines
Roxas Avenue, Manila
tel: 2 832 1125
www.culturalcenter.gov.ph

El Nido Marine Reserve
(*see* page 34)
Plaza Indepedencia
Cebu City
tel: 0919 422 6974
Open Mon–Fri 08:00–12:00,
13:30–17:30, Sat 08:00–12:00

Fort Santiago (*see* page 60)
Callé Santa Clara
Intramuros
Manila
tel: 2 527 1572
Open daily 08:00–16:00

Ifugao Rice Terraces Conservation Heritage Office
Provincial Local Government
Office
Lagawe
tel: 74 382 2108

Kabayan Museum
Kabayan Village
tel: 0908 603 0594
Open Tue–Sat 08:00–12:00,
13:00–17:00

Marcos Museum and Mausoleum
(*see* page 75)
Barangay Lacub, Batac
Open daily 09:00–12:00,
13:00–16:00

Marikina Shoe Museum
(see page 75)
Calle Rizal
Santa Elena, Marikina
tel: 2 430 9735
Open Mon–Fri 10:00–17:00

National Parks of the Philippines
Department of the Environment
and Natural Resources
Visayas Avenue
Diliman, 1100 Quezon City
tel: 2 929 6626
www.denr.gov.ph

Olango Island Wildlife Sanctuary
Ferries from Angasil on the east
coast of Mactan run 05:30–18:00

**Philippine Eagle Research and
Nature Center** (see page 20)
Magalos
Caliman, Davao
tel: 82 224 3021
Open daily 08:00–17:00

**Philippine Institute of
Volcanology and Seismology**
(see page 30)
PHILVOLC Building, CP Garcia Ave
UP Campus, Diliman
Quezon City
tel: 2 426 1468
www.phivolcs.dost.gov.ph

Rizal Museum (see page 75)
Talisay Island
Zamboanga del Norte
Open Tue–Sun 08:00–17:00

Rizal Shrine (see page 75)
Calle Rizal (Calle Real)
Calamba

tel: 919 501 3748
Open Tue–Sun 08:00–12:00,
13:00–17:00

Rizal Shrine
Fort Santiago, Intramuros
tel: 2 527 2961
Open daily 08:00–12:00,
13:00–17:00

**St Paul's Underground River
National Park** (see page 31)
Puerto Princesa, Palawan
tel: 48 433 2409
Open daily 08:00–15:00

Tabon Caves (see page 171)
Tickets and guide obtained from
the Quezon Museum, Quezon City
(signposted off the main street).

Tam-Awan Cultural Village
Pinsao Proper, Baguio
tel: 74 446 2949
www.tamawanvillage.com
Open daily 08:00–18:00 or later
depending on activities

Tarsier Sanctuary (see page 19)
Corella, Bohol
tel: 192 516 3375
Open daily 08:00–16:00

Temple of the 9th Heaven
(see page 70)
Beverley Hills, Cebu City
Open daily 07:00–17:00

**Ylagen de la Rosa Ancestral
Home**
Marcela Agoncillo Street
Taal City
Not regularly open to the public

Activity Companies
Carlos Celdran hosts costumed
walking tours of Intramuros, plus
guided routes in other parts of the
city. The man will open your eyes
to this oft misunderstood city.
Unit 24, North Syquia Aprts
1991 MH de Pilar
Malate, Manila
tel: 2 484 4945
www.celdrantours.blogspot.com

Corregidor
Sun Cruise
Ferry crossing to Corregidor and/or
guided tour of the island.
Hoverferry terminal (by the
Cultural Center of the Philippines)
Roxas Avenue, Manila
tel: 2 831 8140

Whale Watching
(see page 169)
**Pamilacan Island Dolphin and
Whale Watching Tours**
Public Market
Baclayon, Bohol
tel: 38 540 9279

Adventure Windsurfing
(see page 163)
Windsurfing training and rental.
Bulabog Beach, Boracay
tel: 36 288 3182
www.adventure-windsurfing-
boracay.com

Isla Kiteboarding
(see page 162)
Kiteboarding training and rental.
Bulabog Beach, Boracay
tel: 36 288 5352
www.islakite.com

Adventure Sports

Tribal Adventures
Kayaking, rafting, trekking, biking
and expeditions across the country.
New World Renaissance Hotel
Corner of Makati Avenue and
Arniaz Avenue
Makati
Metro Manila
tel: 2 752 7575
www.tribaladventures.com (also
offices on Boracay)

Marsman Drysdale Travel
Offers cultural, bird-watching and
adventure-sports tours around the
country.
19th Floor
Robinsons Summit Center
6783 Ayala Ave
Makati
Metro Manila
tel: 2 887 0000
www.marsman-tours.com.ph

Planet Action
Hiking, caving and general adventure sports on Cebu.
Panagsama Beach
Moaloal, Cebu
tel: 916 624 8253
www.action-philippines.com

Diving

Ananyana (*see* page 117)

Calypso Diving
Boracay
tel: 36 288 3206
www.calypso-asia.com

**Shangri-La Mactan Island Resort
& Spa** (*see* page 106)

Whitewater Rafting

(*see* page 157)
Chico River Quest
P.O. Box Bulanao
Tabuk, Kalinga Province
tel: 922 889 0525
www.chicoriverquest.com

Rafting Cagayan de Oro
112 17th Street
Nazaareth
Cagayan de Oro
tel: 88 857 7238
www.raftingcdo.com

Horse Riding

Camp John Hay (*see* page 154)

Spas

Chi at Shangri-La (*see* page 157)

Ananyana (*see* page 160)

Boracay Regency (*see* page 160)

Mandala Spa (*see* page 160)
Station 3, Boracay
tel: 36 288 5856
www.mandalaspa.com

Nurture Tropical Spa (*see* page 160)
Pulong Sagingan
Barangay Maitim II West
Tagaytay
tel: 46 413 0804

The Farm at San Benito
(*see* page 160)
P.O. Box 39676
119 Barangay Tipakan
Lipa City
tel: 2 884 8074
www.thefarm.com.ph

Golf (*see* pages 172–173)

Intramuros Golf Club
Bonifacio Drive, Manila
tel: 2 527 2887

Camp John Hay
Baguio
tel: 74 442 7902

**Fairways and Bluewater Resort
Golf and Country Club**
Balabag, Boracay
tel: 928 329 9169
www.fairwaysbluewater.com

Luisita Golf Club
Hacienda Luisita, Tarlac
tel: 2 817 9309

Puerto Azul Golf Course
Ternate, Cavite
tel: 46 522 9385

Royal Northwoods Golf Club
San Rafael, Bulacan
tel: 2 443 1656

Sherwood Hills Golf Club
Barangay Cabezas
Cavite
tel: 46 419 0578

**Tagaytay Highlands International
Golf Club**
Tagaytay Highlands, Cavite
tel: 46 483 2639
www.tagaytayhighlands.com

Wack Wack Golf and Country Club
Shaw Boulevard
Mandaluyong City, Metro Manila
tel: 2 723 0665
www.wackwack.com

Casinos and Racetracks

Casino Filipino (*see* page 172)
The Heritage Hotel
Roxas Boulevard, corner EDSA
Pasay City, Manila
tel: 2 854 6848
www.millenniumhotels.com

Hyatt Hotel & Casino
(*see* page 172)
1588 Pedro Gil, corner MH del Pilar
Malate, Manila
tel: 2 245 1234
www.hyatt.com

Waterfront Cebu City Hotel and Casino (*see* page 172)
1 Salinas Drive
Lahug, Cebu City
tel: 32 232 6888
www.waterfronthotels.com.ph

Waterfront Airport Hotel and Casino (*see* page 172)
1 Airport Road
Lapu-Lapu City, Mactan Island
tel: 32 340 5862
www.waterfronthotels.com.ph

Fort Ilocandia Hotel
(*see* page 172)
Barangay 37
Calayab, Laoag, Ilocos Norte
tel: 77 772 1166
www.fortilocandia.com.ph

Fontana Casino (*see* page 172)
Fontana Leisure Parks
CM Recto Highway
Clark Special Economic Zone
Pampanga
tel: 2 843 8798
www.fontanaleisureparks.com

Santa Ana Park (*see* page 172)
AP Reyes Avenue
Makati
Metro Manila
tel: 2 890 4015 or 2 897 9257
(on race days)
www.santa-ana-park.com

Shopping

SM Malls (*see* page 133)
Has 28 malls across the
country.
For more details go to
www.smprime.com

Tiendesitas (*see* page 132)
Ortigas Avenue
corner E Rodriguez Avenue
Manila
tel: 2 635 5680
www.tiendesitas.com.ph

About Design (*see* page 128)
Ground Floor
Greenbelt 3
Makati
Metro Manila
tel: 2 729 9198

B at Home (*see* page 128)
225 Nicaor Garcia Street
Bel Air II
Makati
Metro Manila
tel: 2 896 3616

The Silahis Center (*see* page 133)
744 Callé Real del Palacio
(General Luna)
Intramuros
Manila
tel: 2 527 1314
www.sihalis.com

Alegre Guitars
Barengay Abuño
Lapu-Lapu City
Mactan Island
Cebu
tel: 32 340 4492

Marikina City Hall (*see* page 127)
For outlet mall tours.
tel: 632 646 2360 ext 207

Piña Village (*see* page 133)
Contact the Office of the
Municipal Mayor.
Municipal Building
Magsaysay Park, Kalibo
tel: 36 268 2158

La Herminia Piña Weaving
Old Buswang
Kalibo
tel: 36 262 3797
www.laherminiaweaving.com.ph

Kultura Filipino (*see* page 133)
Stores at the following malls in
Manila – SM Megamall, SM Mall
of Asia, SM Makati Annex, SM
North EDSA The Block and at
selected SM Department Stores.

Jewelmer (*see* page 133)
Has offices in Manila at The
Peninsula Hotel, Makati Shangri-La
Hotel, Glorietta Mall, EDSA
Shangri-La Hotel, SM Megamall
and the Ayala Center in Cebu City.
Head office, Room 701
National Life Insurance Building
6762 Ayala Avenue
Makati, Metro Manila
tel: 2 810 0266
www.jewelmer.com

First edition published in 2008
by New Holland Publishers (UK) Ltd
London • Cape Town • Sydney • Auckland
10 9 8 7 6 5 4 3 2 1

website: www.newhollandpublishers.com

Garfield House, 86 Edgware Road
London W2 2EA
United Kingdom

80 McKenzie Street
Cape Town 8001
South Africa

Unit 1, 66 Gibbes Street,
Chatswood, NSW 2067
Australia

218 Lake Road
Northcote, Auckland
New Zealand

Distributed in the USA by
The Globe Pequot Press
Connecticut

Copyright © 2008 in text: Lindsay Bennett
Copyright © 2008 in maps: Globetrotter Travel Maps
Copyright © 2008 in photographs:
Individual photographers as credited (right).
Copyright © 2008 New Holland Publishers (UK) Ltd

ISBN 978 1 84537 962 9

This guidebook has been written by independent authors and updaters. The information therein represents their impartial opinion, and neither they nor the publishers accept payment in return for including in the book or writing more favourable reviews of any of the establishments. Whilst every effort has been made to ensure that this guidebook is as accurate and up to date as possible, please be aware that the facts quoted are subject to change, particularly the price of food, transport and accommodation. The Publisher accepts no responsibility or liability for any loss, injury or inconvenience incurred by readers or travellers using this guide.

Publishing Manager: Thea Grobbelaar
DTP Cartographic Manager: Genené Hart
Editor: Carla Zietsman
Design and DTP: Nicole Bannister
Cartographer: Nicole Bannister
Picture Researchers: Zainoenisa Manuel, Shavonne Govender
Illustrator: Tanja Spinola
Consultant: Nigel Hicks
Proofreader: Thea Grobbelaar

Reproduction by Resolution, Cape Town
Printed and bound in China by C & C Offset Printing Co., Ltd.

Acknowledgments:
The author wishes to thank Mariano Garchitorena for his enthusiasm, friendship and seemingly endless list of contacts, and Rene Gualto and Gemma Batoon for their help and guidance.

Photographic Credits:
Amanpulo Hotel: pages 118, 120, 161;
Ananyana Hotel: page 117;
Pete Bennett: cover page, half title page, pages 8–9, 10, 18, 22–23, 25, 26, 32–33, 36–37, 42, 44–45, 48–49, 50, 53, 56, 61, 62, 63, 66, 68–69, 72–73, 74, 76–77, 85, 86, 90, 93, 98, 100–101, 102, 104, 106, 113, 115, 122–123, 127, 129, 130, 131, 132, 134–135, 136, 138, 140, 143, 144, 148–149, 150, 155, 156, 162, 164, 168, 170, 174–175, 176, 179;
David Bowden: pages 6, 19, 46, 171;
Tom Cockrem: pages 82–83, 96, 133;
El Nido Resorts: page 110;
Nigel Hicks: contents page, pages 16, 17, 21, 28–29, 31, 35, 38–39, 64–65, 78, 94, 152, 167;
JD Martin: title page, pages 40, 79;
Picture Press/Photo Access: pages 14–15, 158–159;
Pictures Colour Library: pages 71, 124, 139, 145;
Shangri-La Hotel: pages 107, 146–147;
Sime/Photo Access: pages 12, 172
Travel Pix Collection/jonarnoldimages: page 43

Keep us Current
Information in travel guides is apt to change, which is why we regularly update our guides. We'd be grateful to receive feedback if you've noted something we should include in our updates. If you have new information, please share it with us by writing to the Publishing Manager, Globetrotter, at the office nearest to you (addresses on this page). The most significant contribution to each new edition will receive a free copy of the updated guide.

Cover: *Duljo Beach, Panglao Island.*
Half title: *Sunset on White Beach, Boracay Island.*
Title page: *Local children on boat, Boracay Island.*
Contents page: *Typical boat, Apo Island.*